# ALL OF
# GRACE

# CHARLES H.
# SPURGEON

**Bridge-Logos**
Newberry, FL 32669-2765 USA

## Bridge-Logos

Newberry, FL 32669-2765 USA

*All of Grace*
by Charles H. Spurgeon

Copyright © 2007 by Bridge-Logos

Printed in the United States of America.

Library of Congress Catalog Card Number: 2006927585
International Standard Book Number: 978-0-88270-335-0

Scripture quotations are from the *King James Version* of the Bible.

BP 04-19-16

# Contents

# Charles Haddon Spurgeon
## 1834-1892

*From Boy Preacher to Prince of Preachers, Charles Haddon Spurgeon moved tens of thousands to trust Christ for their eternal salvation and left a treasure trove of sermons and writings that continue to move and touch his readers. And Spurgeon did all through great infirmities and trials, living humbly even as he became a world-renowned celebrity.*

The 15-year-old boy entered the Primitive Methodist Church amid a howling snowstorm that had kept him from reaching his intended church. The unusual English storm also kept the preacher from reaching the church. Only a handful of hearty believers made it, and the young lad, Charles, joined them in the service with singing.

Charles describes the events this way:

> "At last, a very thin looking man, a shoemaker, went up into the pulpit to preach … He was forced to stick to his Scripture text, for the simple reason that he had little else to say. The text was, 'Look unto me, and be ye saved, all the ends of the earth' (Isaiah 45:22).
>
> "When he had managed to spin out ten minutes or so, he was at the end of his tether. Then he looked at me under the gallery, and I daresay, with so few present, he knew me to be a stranger. Just fixing his eyes on me, as if he knew all my heart, he said, 'Young man, you look very miserable.' Well, I did, but I had not been accustomed to have remarks made from the pulpit on my personal appearance before. However, it was a good blow, struck right home. He continued, 'And you always will be miserable—miserable in life, and miserable in death—if you don't obey my text; but if you obey now,

this moment, you will be saved.' Then, lifting up his hands, he shouted as only a Primitive Methodist could do, 'Young man, look to Jesus Christ. Look! Look! Look! You have nothing to do but to look and live.'

"I saw at once the way of salvation … I had been waiting to do fifty things, but when I heard the word, 'Look!' what a charming word it seemed to me! Oh! I looked until I could almost have looked my eyes away. There and then the cloud was gone, the darkness had rolled away, and that moment I saw the sun; and I could have risen that instant, and sung with the most enthusiastic of them, of the precious blood of Christ, and the simple faith which looks alone to HIM …

> E'er since by faith I saw the stream
> Thy flowing wounds supply
> Redeeming love has been my theme
> And shall be till I die."

God's hand was in a snowstorm, an absent preacher, a faithful little shoemaker, and an aptly spoken word. And He brought forth the salvation of a man who would see tens of thousands of souls converted under his ministry, and tens of millions influenced by his writings that are reprinted and absorbed by Christians to this day. Once in the Kingdom, God lit a fire in Charles that would light the way for millions of people.

The bedraggled fifteen-year-old boy who heard the word of the Lord that day and looked up to see Jesus was Charles Haddon Spurgeon, often called the Prince of Preachers, a teacher and man who lived the Word and was used by God.

### Young Beginnings

Spurgeon's Christian roots can be traced back to persecuted Dutchmen who fled to England centuries earlier only to find different persecution. Job Spurgeon was imprisoned in 1677 for six years and had all of his belongings confiscated for attending a worship service not sanctioned by the Church of England. A few years after being released from prison, he was sent back for the same offense.

Spurgeon's father and grandfather were both strong Christians and Congregationalist ministers.

Into this godly heritage, Charles Haddon Spurgeon was born June 19, 1834 in Kelvedon, Essex, England—the first of seventeen children. Interestingly, as an infant, he was sent to live with his grandparents and stayed with them until he was six years old. There, he was given a complete youngster's understanding of Scriptures, and by age six he had learned to love John Bunyan's classic Pilgrim's Progress.

Back with his parents, he grew up in a home with strong Puritan teachings and faithful, restrained lives to match. There was no known hypocrisy in his parents' lives. And the Spurgeons did not allow it in their offspring. By outward standards, he and his siblings were exemplary children.

Little Charles once lost his pencil and decided to buy one at the store on credit. When his father found out, he gave him a lecture on the sins of debt that he never forgot.

> "I was marched off to the shop like a deserter marched into barracks, crying bitterly all down the street and feeling dreadfully ashamed, because I thought everybody knew I was in debt. The farthing was paid amid solemn warnings, and the poor debtor was set free like a bird out of a cage."

Spurgeon spent some time at a boarding school, and here we see a flash of his occasional fieriness. When he first started there, he knelt to pray before going to bed and was pelted by other boys with slippers and other items. He arose and struck at the mocking boys to his right and then to his left. After several were knocked down, the others stopped and stayed still. Then he knelt back down and returned to his prayers. He reported not being interrupted again.

From his earliest days, Spurgeon struggled with the sin in his life. Although his sinfulness might appear small from the outside, it weighed heavily on the boy's heart. No doubt at least part of this reason was all the talk and teaching in the home of fallen nature. In addition to Scripture, Spurgeon was reared on the writings of John Bunyan and Richard Baxter, making him keenly aware of the soul's struggle with sin. He had a sharp sense of the justice of God.

> "Sin, whatever it might be to other people, became to me an intolerable burden. It was not so much that I feared hell as that I feared sin, and all the while I had upon my mind a deep concern for the honour of God's name. I felt that it would not satisfy my conscience if I could be forgiven unjustly, but then there came the question, how could God be just and yet justify me, who had been so guilty?"

During that cold Sunday morning in January 1850, Spurgeon was making his way toward his own church, but the fateful snowstorm forced him to the Primitive Methodist Church where the faithful cobbler showed him the way to salvation through the words of the prophet Isaiah.

Spurgeon, of course, knew the Gospel well from his upbringing, but God chose to use a vehicle outside his family to draw him to His Son. It was the longing of his heart, and Christ filled it.

> "I do from my soul confess that I was never satisfied till I came to Christ ... Since that dear hour when my soul cast itself on Jesus, I have found solid joy and peace, but before that all those supposed gaieties of early youth, all the imagined joy and ease of boyhood, were but vanity and vexation of spirit to me. That happy day when I found the Saviour and learnt to cling to His dear feet was a day never to be forgotten by me, an obscure child, unknown, unheard of. I listened to

the word of God, and that precious text led me to the Cross of Christ."

Spurgeon attended Oxford for a while. However, because he was not a member of the Church of England, he was not allowed to earn a degree. But he studied diligently, and his keen mind was obvious. And he was free to preach as he desired, taking part in street preaching.

Spurgeon was never able to keep his joy and the basic message of the Gospel to himself. It spilled out of him naturally. Almost immediately, he set out as a servant of God, putting his hand to the plow and not looking back. There was nothing too small or trivial; he only wanted to do God's will. The Lord began him small, found him faithful, and in a stunningly short time, brought him to great things.

> "The very first service which my youthful heart rendered to Christ was the placing of tracts in envelopes, and then sealing them up, that I might send them. I might have done nothing for Christ if I had not been encouraged by finding myself able to do a little. Then I sought to do something more, and from that something more, and I do not doubt that many servants of God have been led on to higher and nobler labours for their Lord, because they began to serve Him in the right spirit and manner."

His spirit was to share Christ in any way he could—writing verses on a scrap of paper and leaving it for someone to find.

> "I could scarcely content myself even for five minutes without trying to do something for Christ."

Nothing could stop him.

> "It may be that in the young dawn of my Christian life, I did imprudent things in order to serve the cause

of Christ, but I still say, give me back that time again, with all its imprudence and with all its hastiness, if I may but have the same love to my Master, the same overwhelming influence in my spirit, making me obey my Lord's commands because it was a pleasure to me to do anything to serve my God."

### Deceived Onto the Path of Greatness

Spurgeon was actually tricked into his first sermon. James Vinter, who headed the Local Preachers' Association in Cambridge, heard of Spurgeon's success giving the closing address after Sunday school. Vinter invited Spurgeon to accompany a man to the village of Teversham where he was to preach. Enroute, Spurgeon said he would be praying for him, and the man stopped in surprise. He had never preached, he said, and never intended to. He assumed Spurgeon was preaching and suggested that if he were not, they should turn back.

Spurgeon realized he had been tricked, but he decided to give a message anyway, even though he was completely unprepared and had never preached. He chose the Scripture "Unto you therefore which believe He is precious" on which to preach, and God greatly blessed the sixteen-year-old. When he finished, a woman's voice piped up and asked, "Bless your dear heart. How old are you?" Spurgeon very solemnly replied, "You must wait till the service is over before making such inquiries. Let us now sing."

And so the boy preacher was launched at sixteen.

Within eighteen months of his conversion, Spurgeon was made pastor of the small Waterbeach Baptist Chapel.

He said he became a Baptist because of studying the New Testament in Greek. "According to my reading of Holy Scripture, the believer in Christ should be buried with Him in baptism, and so enter upon his open Christian life."

Spurgeon's mother once proclaimed, "Ah, Charles! I often prayed the Lord to make you a Christian, but I never asked that you become a Baptist."

Spurgeon with a smile responded quickly, "Ah, mother! The Lord has answered your prayer with His usual bounty, and given you exceeding abundantly above what you asked or thought."

England was in a state of considerable spiritual darkness, with corruption and apathy in the Church of England. While there were firm remnants of Christianity, the overall picture was dismal. The Rev. Desmond Morse-Boycott of the Church of England wrote:

> "England was a land of closed churches and unstoled clergy ... The parson was often an absentee, not infrequently a drunkard ... The rich went to church to doze in upholstered curtained pews fitted with fireplaces, while the poor were herded together on uncomfortable benches."

The small town of Waterbeach was in a similarly, spiritually dilapidated state. But God was with the seventeen-year-old pastor, and the work of Charles Spurgeon began to bear fruit almost immediately. The thatched-roof church was soon crammed with people, and some men who were the lowest and most noxious in the village became great blessings in the church.

Many of the villagers helped out their young pastor with his needs, knowing that the tiny amount of income he was provided could not support even such a modest lifestyle. Spurgeon was determined to stick it out as long as God desired it. He seemed to want little for himself and truly delighted in the changed lives of those in the village.

> "I can testify that great numbers of humble country folk accepted the Saviour's invitation, and it was delightful to see what a firm grip they afterwards had on the verities of the faith. Many of them became perfect masters of divinity. I used to think sometimes that if they had degrees who deserved them, diplomas would often be transferred and given to those who hold the plough handle or work at the carpenter's bench."

This attitude toward the simple man remained with Spurgeon, a country boy himself, who remained comfortable and approachable by any class even when he became a worldwide name.

He spent three years in Waterbeach and although a mere teenager most of the time, the church and the village flourished under his care and ministering. He wrote:

> "It was a pleasant thing to walk through that place when drunkenness had almost ceased, when debauchery in the case of many was dead, when men and women went forth to labour with joyful hearts, singing the praises of the ever-living God."

### New Park Street: Great Church, Little Preacher

In November 1853, the young man received an invitation to preach a Sunday service at New Park Street Chapel in London. New Park Street was famous among Baptists and Londoners and most Christians as a place of great godly influence and preaching in the 1700s. Spurgeon thought at first it was a mistake. Why would such a great church be interested in this little, country lay preacher?

But after he determined that the invitation was indeed not an error, he replied in sincere humility, informing them that he was only nineteen and had never preached in a large church. He went on to say he had a prior commitment for the date they requested and offered December 11. The New Park Street deacons accepted.

New Park Street Chapel was symbolic of the decline in Baptist churches in England in the middle 1800s. The once vibrant church was a shell of its former glory. Few congregations in the whole of London topped three hundred people, and all the talk was of the decline in church attendance. In fact, the Baptist denomination was divided on several issues.

Spurgeon arrived in London on a cold and dreary day, staying in a tiny little apartment where the other young men boarding there ridiculed him for claiming that he would be preaching at New Park Street. He felt completely alone, without a friend in the city. When he tried to sleep, it was torture in the cramped room with the cacophony of horses and cabs all night. He already hated London.

And yet he considered that perhaps God was in all of it.

When he arrived at New Park Street the next morning, he was in awe of the magnificent building, and wondered how such a sophisticated and perhaps critical congregation would receive him. But more surprises were in store. As the time of the service approached, the great chapel did not fill up. In fact, it was dotted with just a few souls. It felt practically empty.

Spurgeon rose and spoke on "Every good gift and every perfect gift is from above and cometh down from the Father of Lights, with Whom is no variableness neither shadow of turning." Every thread of Spurgeon's preaching led up to the Cross. He did not preach on moral issues or anything in modern debate. He simply preached Christ crucified and let everything else fall as it may.

The people seemed unsure of the young preacher who knew Scripture so well and seemed to already have a vast wealth of knowledge and experience. But when the evening service came about, everyone returned and brought a good number more with them. He preached from Revelation, "They are without fault before the throne of God."

In one day, his future and the church's future were cemented together. He was invited to pastor the church. And while he could not accept immediately, and did not treasure leaving his flock in Waterbeach, he received peace from God to take the position.

### Spurgeon Breaks the Mold

Spurgeon was not one to simply go with the flow. But he also understood the need for discipline and submission.

An example from his first months at New Park Street Chapel demonstrates this vividly. He was not truly ordained when he accepted the New Park Street pulpit. It was suggested there be a formal ordination service over which one of London's ordained ministers would preside. Spurgeon thoughtfully replied in a long letter to the deacons.

He opposed the ordination ceremony. His calling was from God, and He had already recognized his ministry. He objected to the concept of ministers passing on power from one to another and believed it was completely up to the local church. But, he was willing to submit to the church leadership if they felt his ceremonial ordination to be critically important: "It will be submission. I shall endure it as a self-mortification in order that you may all be pleased. I would rather please you than myself."

The ordination ceremony never took place.

Spurgeon also broke the mold of tradition by discouraging references to himself as "Reverend" or even "Pastor," and by discarding the long, black frock of ministers and wearing plain clothes. These changes were severely criticized by other ministers, who believed they ought to be set apart from the flock. Moreover, Spurgeon broke through the heavy academic style of preaching so in vogue. He chose instead to speak directly to his listeners in words that could not possibly be misunderstood.

But it was not the insistence on outward changes that brought people to hear Spurgeon; it was the message of Jesus Christ crucified and arisen, and the need for Him alone for salvation. And the people came and came. Soon, not only was the once nearly empty chapel filled, but the street outside was blocked on Sundays for the overflow crowd to listen to this very young man of God.

Soon it became evident that larger space was necessary. They turned to the Music Hall in the Royal Surrey Gardens. This was a huge step, because the building housed up to 12,000 people. Spurgeon and William Olney—the man who was instrumental in bringing Spurgeon to London—feared it might have been far too large and they would have looked silly. But where they were simply could not work any longer, so they pressed forward.

### Terror, Flight, Disorder and Death

It was a disaster that first night in October 1856. The Music Hall was jammed to capacity, such as it never was with secular performances. But after a Scripture reading and prayer, the wicked had their planned moment. Someone shouted, "Fire!" and another shouted, "The balcony is giving way!" Several others shouted similar fears. A panic erupted among the people and as they pressed toward the doors, seven people were killed, trampled by others desperately trying to flee a perfectly safe building.

*The British Banner* wrote: "At the most solemn moment of the occasion, the wicked rose in their strength, like a whirlwind, sin entered, followed by terror, flight, disorder and death!"

It seemed clear to everyone that it was a staged effort by evil-doers to wreck the work of God—everyone except Spurgeon, who to the end of his life wanted to "hope there was no concerted wickedness."

Spurgeon, only twenty-two years old, was devastated. The burden of it overwhelmed him. He became sick and was unable to preach for a couple of Sundays. But gradually his strength returned, and along with it his speaking became as powerful as ever. And the church was able to make good use of Music Hall afterward.

Eventually, however, a new building of their own was needed. In 1861, they built the Metropolitan Tabernacle, which still stands in London today. It was a huge structure that comfortably seated 3,700, with room for another 2,000 to squeeze in, which they normally did.

### Charles in Love

Susannah Thompson was a "greatly privileged favourite" of William Olney, who was the lead Deacon and responsible for bringing Spurgeon to London. And so she saw Spurgeon preach his first three sermons at New Park Street Chapel.

Despite her Christian upbringing, she had never professed her faith in Christ, although she was very well aware of her need for the Saviour.

During a Sunday evening sermon about a year before Spurgeon arrived, the preacher spoke on "The word is nigh thee, even in thy mouth, and in thy heart," and the light dawned in Susannah's soul. She wrote:

"The Lord said to me, through His servant, 'Give me thine heart,' and, constrained by His love, that night witnessed my solemn resolution of entire surrender to Himself."

But she records that she grew cold and indifferent to the things of God, and was in such a state when Spurgeon took the pulpit.

Some of their early connections are shrouded in personal privacy that eludes history. But she writes that quite unexpectedly, Spurgeon gave her an illustrated copy of *The Pilgrim's Progress*, the John Bunyan book that had meant so much to him since childhood. He inscribed it, "Miss Thompson, with desires for progress in the blessed pilgrimage, from C.H. Spurgeon, April 20, 1854."

In June 1854, the two were providentially seated next to each other at a party. Spurgeon handed a book written by Martin Tupper to Susannah and asked about a quotation in it: "Seek a good wife of Thy God, for she is the best gift of His Providence."

She blushed slightly, then heard him whisper the question, "Do you pray for him who is to be your husband?" There was a pause, and then Spurgeon asked her if she would take a walk with him. In August, they were engaged and they married on January 8, 1856.

The home they made was modest, and they took care to avoid any excessive displays. Their homes in town and later in Westwood were seemingly open to everyone: to missionaries, preachers and visitors from around the world. And they gave generously to those in need. The estimates from a review of their accounting books found that they gave away about five times as much as they kept for themselves. That's more than an eighty percent "tithe."

The Spurgeon's twin boys—Thomas and Charles—were born September 20, 1856. They were tremendous blessings to their parents and became preachers and leading men of God themselves. But the birth left Susannah an invalid in her home for fifteen years. Yet her joy and that of her husband did not diminish.

"She was a fine example of the triumph of sanctified will over physical suffering," J.C. Carlile wrote in *Charles Spurgeon, The Great Orator*. "Even in pain, she dictated many letters to other sufferers and helped bear the burdens of ministries of all denominations who had fallen on evil times."

Out of the money she saved in frugal housekeeping, she began the Book Fund, which financed thousands of books of Bible study for pastors around the world. She also found money for soup kitchens, clothing for the children of poorly paid village ministers, and the individual needs of untold numbers of people.

Despite her fragile health, Susannah proved to be the ideal partner for Spurgeon, loving and serving the Lord first and sharing a spiritual intensity that helped buoy him when he needed it. Despite her extended illness, she did not seem to be a major burden on her husband. On the contrary, she was his helpmate.

## Prince of Preachers

Spurgeon brought a whole new method to preaching. He did not strive for the flowery speech of the humanists or the rhetoric of the High Calvinists. Nor did he muddle through, as did many of the rural preachers. He spoke simply and from the depth of his heart and his intellect, but it was not to impress man. It was to impress upon man the glory of God, the fallen sinning state of each of us and the salvation of Christ.

"His ideal was that of the fisherman," wrote Carlile, who was a student under Spurgeon. "He lowered his net to catch fish; he baited his hook, not for decorative purposes but to secure souls."

Spurgeon never took his eye off the Word. God's great truths defined everything for him, and they informed his preaching. He wanted to make people clearly understand him. There would be no fogs in his preaching.

"Sermons should have real teaching in them, and their doctrine should be solid, substantial and abundant," Spurgeon wrote. "The world still needs to be told of its Saviour and of the way to reach Him."

Spurgeon did not do much on the spur of the moment. Occasionally he gave sermons without preparation—such as his first one. But most of the time he was intent on always finding just the right words and meanings to make his point clear. He wanted to use illustrations to make the points from ancient Scripture real to his listeners. He was very willing to quote other great men of God, from Bunyan to John Knox to Richard Baxter. And so he labored over every sermon, always starting at the beginning—with prayer. In speaking to students at his Pastors' College, he put it very clearly to them:

"I frequently sit hour after hour praying and waiting for a subject, and this is the main part of my study; much hard labour have I spent in manipulating topics, ruminating upon points of doctrine, making skeletons out of verses and then burying every bone of them in the catacombs of oblivion, sailing on and on over leagues of broken water till I see the red lights and make sail direct to the desired haven.

"Unstudied thoughts coming from the mind without previous research, without the subjects in hand having been investigated at all, must be of a very inferior quality, even from the most superior men, and as none of us would have the effrontery to glorify ourselves as men of genius or wonders of erudition, I fear that our unpremeditated thoughts upon most subjects would not be remarkably worthy of attention at all.

"Our sermons should be our mental lifeblood—the outflow of our intellectual and spiritual vigor; or, to change the figure, they should be diamonds well cut and well set, precious intrinsically and bearing the marks of labour. God forbid that we should offer to the Lord that which costs us nothing."

And there you have the heart of C.H. Spurgeon on preaching. Notice that it does not include anything other than what is driving the preacher to preach. There is nothing on methods or deliveries or services. Where is the heart of the man expounding on the Word of God? That was the question for Spurgeon.

When asked once about how he attracted so many people while other churches were dormant or dwindling, he answered:

"I did not seek them. They have always sought me. My concern has been to preach Christ and leave the rest to His keeping."

That was his heart.

Although it would not be his style, Spurgeon could certainly point to the results of preaching Christ first and Him crucified, preaching from deep study and prayer, and preaching for the glory of the Lord and not the preacher.

## The Tabernacle For a Growing Congregation

The church needed a new home, and although the Music Hall worked for a while, the leadership knew that they needed to build. Spurgeon's vision was for a Greek structure. He felt there were no sacred languages other than ancient Greek and Hebrew. He believed that a Christian church should not be a Gothic structure, but should be Grecian.

The Metropolitan Tabernacle was completed in 1861—the largest church in the world at the time, holding nearly 6,000 people. Predictably, Spurgeon was criticized for building such a monumental edifice. He was charged with puffing himself up and being ostentatious. It was also said that the money could have been better spent on the poor. But the charges of egotism and ostentation evaporated when the church opened and filled up twice every Sunday. And as for helping the poor, Spurgeon's personal giving and books open for review shamed any critic. The couple's eighty percent tithe put to rest the lie that he was making himself rich through the Tabernacle.

At one point, an American lecture bureau invited him to come to America to tour all major cities and give fifty lectures. They offered to pay all expenses, plus $50,000—which would be a quarter million dollars today. Spurgeon wasn't interested. Ever keeping his eye on the Master's will, he quickly replied, "I can do better. I will stay in London and try to save fifty souls."

He was comfortable, but given his position of worldwide prominence and influence, and particularly the sales of millions of his books, his lifestyle was very modest. He could have lived as a king, but lived *for* the King and allowed his riches to be stored up in heaven rather than on earth.

### Winning Souls From His Knees

Spurgeon did not desire to take church members from other congregations; he wanted to get the lost into the Tabernacle and into the Kingdom. By always preaching Christ and salvation, he knew he never missed the opportunity for a lost soul to hear the Gospel.

The soul-winning ways of Spurgeon began where everything began with him: in prayer. The Tabernacle was known as a church that prayed. Spurgeon may have set the example for many in later years, but the leadership had made the commitment before he arrived. The remnant that sought him out were on their knees, paving the way. That critical resolution was never lost.

No doubt many people came to hear Spurgeon out of curiosity, but saved or lost, they all heard a Christ preached that captured them.

Bob Ross wrote that Spurgeon "plainly preached the Word, pressing the Law and the Gospel upon his hearers—the Law to convict and break the hardened, and the Gospel to heal the broken."

He loved God and he loved his fellow men. Here is how he concluded one of his sermons:

> "He that believeth not shall be damned. Weary sinner, hellish sinner, thou who are at the devil's castaway, reprobate, profligate, harlot, robber, thief,

adulterer, fornicator, drunkard, swearer ... listen! I speak to thee as to the rest. I exempt no man. God hath said there is no exemption here. Whosoever believeth in the name of Jesus Christ shall be saved. Sin is no barrier. The guilt is no obstacle. Whosoever, though he were black as Satan, though he were guilty as a fiend—whosoever this night believes shall every sin forgiven, shall every crime effaced, shall every iniquity blotted out; shall be saved in the Lord Jesus Christ, and shall stand in heaven safe and secure. That is the glorious gospel. God apply it home to your hearts and give you faith in Jesus."

New Park Street went from 232 members when Spurgeon arrived to more than 5,000 about ten years later. It was the largest independent congregation in the world—independent of denominations, but dependent on the King of kings. Prime Minister Gladstone, many members of the royal family, members of Parliament, and dignitaries from around the world visited the Tabernacle. But no matter who was in attendance, like Baxter and others before him, the message had to remain the same. All were sinners; all needed Christ or were condemned eternally. No one from the rag-tag orphan to the king escaped the equation.

People swarmed to him to hear the Truth. No numbers were kept, because Spurgeon did not use the modern altar call. He did not request a public decision. He simply quoted Scripture to believe in Christ and be saved. But even without the numbers, the fruits were quite clear. The growth of the church was primarily new believers. He planted several other churches in the London area, offshoots of the Tabernacle.

"From the very early days of my ministry in London, the Lord gave such an abundant blessing upon the proclamation of His truth that whenever I was able to appoint a time for seeking converts and inquirers, it was seldom, if ever, that I waited in vain; and usually, so many came, that I was quite overwhelmed with gratitude and thanksgiving to God."

## Spurgeon's Legacy of the Pen

Spurgeon always loved to write. As a child, he planned his own magazine and wrote articles for it. This gift carried on until his death, leaving a godly legacy to future generations through both his preaching and writings.

From early on, there was such demand for the words he gave that his sermons were printed and distributed in England and the United States. The first ones were bound up and 500 printed. They disappeared so fast, more were printed until about 6,000 were distributed. Later more than 200,000 booklets with his sermons were printed.

Probably the most popular books he wrote were a little series entitled *John Ploughman's Talk*. More than 300,000 volumes were printed and sold very quickly. Subsequent printings added greatly to that number.

His writings encouraged lay believers and instructed ministers. But mostly, they were meant for the average man.

There was more that Spurgeon accomplished. In 1856 he started the Pastor's College with only one student. It grew steadily until about one hundred young men were enrolled to become ministers of the Gospel. The College also housed the Stockwell Orphanage with boys' and girls' schools overseen by Spurgeon and supported by funds he helped raise.

He published a monthly magazine called the *Sword and the Trowel*, beginning in 1865, in which he essentially continued preaching Christ, but also touched on issues of doctrine within the church.

His autobiography lists seventy-eight books he wrote and published, in addition to the sermons and the magazine.

## Calvinist Without Apology

Spurgeon was an unapologetic Calvinist, in that he believed what Calvin believed. But he disliked the term, because it took the focus off the Saviour. He simply agreed with Calvin's theology, and believed that the Puritan fathers had come closest to Scriptural truth.

"We know nothing of the new ologies; we stand by the old ways ... Believing that the Puritanic school embodied more gospel truth in it than any other since the days of the apostles."

He defined Calvinism in its simplest terms this way:

"If anyone should ask me what I mean by a Calvinist, I should reply, 'He is one who says, Salvation is of the Lord.' I cannot find in Scripture any other doctrine than this. It is the essence of the Bible. 'He only is my rock and my salvation.' Tell me anything contrary to this truth, and it will be heresy; tell me a heresy, and I shall find its essence here, that it has departed from this great, this fundamental rock-truth, 'God is my rock and my salvation.'"

The Protestant pastors were generally evangelical, but they were weak in their doctrine. And the result was clear in the lives of church members. Spurgeon wanted to set the church back on the rock-hard path of strong doctrine.

Spurgeon said:

"My daily labor is to revive the old doctrines of Gill, Owen, Calvin, Augustine and Christ ... The old truth that Calvin preached, that Augustine preached, is the truth that I preach today, or else I would be false to my conscience and my God. I cannot shape truth; I know of no such thing as paring off the rough edges of a doctrine. John Knox's gospel is my gospel. And that gospel which thundered through Scotland must thunder through England again."

In his day, however, not unlike today, there were elements from Hyper-Calvinists to Arminians who found fault with Spurgeon's doctrine. Knowing Scripture so well—he had much of it committed to memory—and knowing the writings of the church fathers intimately, he was able to aptly defend his doctrines.

But while willing to do it, he did not like the arena of battling other believers over issues of doctrine. He preferred the bottom line.

> "If I am asked to say what my creed is, I think I must reply, 'It is Jesus Christ' ... Jesus Christ, Who is the sum and the substance of the Gospel, Who is in Himself all theology, the Incarnation of every precious truth, the all-glorious embodiment of the way, the truth and the life."

He urged listeners, "Do not make minor doctrines main points," but stick with the theme of grace from God through Jesus. Yet he could discuss the most minute doctrines in great detail and earnestness, and they were apparently important to him.

### Battling the Erosion and Corrosion of the Down-Grade

By the late 1880s, there was an insipid falling away from God's Truth that infected many churches, including the Baptists. Some ministers openly preached against the infallibility of the Bible, the deity of Christ and eternal salvation. Those few were censured by the Baptist Union. But many others did so more surreptitiously. In the light of great scientific discoveries, these learned men began to question portions of Scripture or elements of the Trinity. They cast themselves as progressive and modern. Some found a new understanding in the theories of Charles Darwin, and pointed to what they felt were contradictions between Scripture and science—choosing science as their guide. Their congregations followed.

Carlile wrote:

> "The pulpit was charged with silent surrender to the radical betrayal of the evangelical foundations of the Christian faith."

A blind eye was turned toward this apostasy within the Baptist Union and other denominations. It became known as the "Down-Grade" controversy.

Spurgeon at first thought it was an exception here and there. But he soon began to see a rapid spread of these ideas and was alarmed at the sudden infusion within his own denomination. Spurgeon was a very sick man by this point, and in fact, was only a few years from death. He likely knew it. And so there was no personal gain for him to enter into such a burgeoning fray at the end of his life. In fact, it probably taxed his failing strength.

Nonetheless, he felt compelled to defend the Gospel.

After a number of private conversations and correspondences with men he thought were reducing Scripture, and with S.H. Booth, the secretary of the Baptist Union, he brought the issue into the open in an 1887 *Sword and the Trowel* article. In the magazine, he issued a general warning to readers of the defection from the Truth that was riddling the Nonconformist churches.

Spurgeon laid out three charges: 1) The infallibility of Scripture from God was denied, 2) the way of salvation through Christ was not preached, and 3) hell was denied, as was any eternal punishment for sin.

It went right to the heart of the Gospel.

Just how deeply the unbelief had ensnared the church became obvious with the response. Many in the camp of science vigorously attacked Spurgeon over religion. He was also attacked through Christian publications and even the pulpit. And shockingly, at the next annual meeting of the Baptist Union, the issue was ignored. There was complete silence.

After repeated attempts to get the Baptist Union to confront the issue, Spurgeon felt he had no choice. He withdrew from the union. By unanimous vote, the congregation of the Tabernacle followed him. This was a blow to the union, as Spurgeon was by far the best-known Baptist preacher, and his congregation many times larger than any other. After several private attempts to get Spurgeon to return, the union passed a motion of censure against him—almost unanimously.

Booth claimed that Spurgeon had never brought the matter up with him. Spurgeon was stunned and was ready to produce the written documentation between Booth and him as evidence that the matter had indeed been thoroughly explored. But Booth insisted that those were private correspondences. As easily as Spurgeon could have proved his position and Booth's hypocrisy, he honored his old friend, and in spite of the betrayal, never revealed the letters. Without the proof, he undermined his own credibility. He also lost a friend. This was a painful split, because Spurgeon and Booth had been close for many years. To Booth's credit, Spurgeon knew he was trying to keep the controversy from blowing up and dividing the union. But it was unacceptable compromise for Spurgeon.

The censure passed by the Baptist Union was a deep wound for Spurgeon. But he had set out his path of defense of Scripture and would not turn back. He was absolutely militant about God's Word. But however strong his heart was in the matter, his body was not up to the battle. The controversy wore down his feeble frame even further, hastening the inevitable.

### Suffering with Christ

Like so many great men and women of God, Spurgeon tasted of immense physical suffering. And much of his suffering was brought on by his zeal to push himself to the brink and beyond to do God's good will.

Arnold Dallimore wrote of the schedule that took its toll on Spurgeon's body:

> "Although he began full of youthful vigor he labored
> to such an extent that his health soon was drained. He
> preached ten times a week on the average, often in
> places that were far removed from London. He oversaw
> his Pastors' College, his orphanage and almshouses,
> and bore the responsibility of raising the funds to keep
> them all vibrant and healthy. Every Monday he edited a
> sermon preached the previous day to prepare it for the

press and each month he produced his magazine. He was also constantly producing books."

By the age of thirty, he was already showing the signs of the stress. The painful disease of gout developed. Over the years, he would be in such agony that he was bed-ridden and unable to move. Many of his sermons were preached through obvious pain. He would use his cane and, with the help of church members, mount the podium to preach. Frequently, once he embarked upon the word of God, the pain seemed to dissipate, and he became animated and energetic until he was finished.

Spurgeon's views on his physical suffering are not those of many Christians today. He saw suffering as a gift from God. Without his suffering, he never could have been the comforting and sympathetic man that he was to the sick and downtrodden.

His son, Charles Jr., wrote:

"I know of no one who could, more sweetly than my dear father, impart comfort to bleeding hearts and sad spirits. As the crushing of the flower causes it to yield its aroma, so he, having endured in the long continued illness of my beloved mother, and also constant pains himself, was able to sympathize most tenderly with all sufferers."

Spurgeon knew this truth intimately.

"In the matter of faith healing, health is set before us as if it were the great thing to be desired above all things. Is it so? I venture to say that the greatest earthly blessing that God can give to any of us is health, with the exception of sickness. Sickness has frequently been of more use to the saints of God than health has."

### *Spurgeon at Rest, at Last*

In his last years, Spurgeon spent some wintertime in Menton, in South France, to help his ailing body. That is where he was in January 1892. He was very sick, yet he could not help but hold little services with just the handful of friends and family. He had spoken to the great throngs of thousands, but he would expound the word of God to any group, no matter how small.

Wilson Carlile was with Spurgeon in his last days, and it was clear that the Down-Grade issue was still on his heart.

> "When he was dying at the East Bay, Menton, my wife and I went to his family prayers, which he took though in bed. He prayed for all the wandering sheep, concluding, 'Thou, Lord, seest the various labels upon them and rightly regardest them by the mark of the Cross in their hearts. They are all Thy one fold.'"

Spurgeon crossed the River Jordan January 31, 1892, and entered into the loving arms of the Master whom he served so diligently on this earth. Typical of his humility and understanding of man's heart, he had left the request: "Remember, a plain stone. 'C.H.S.' and no more; no fuss."

He knew that a monument would be to him, and not to his Saviour. On his casket was this inscription:

> "In ever loving memory of Charles Haddon Spurgeon, born at Kelvedon, June 19, 1834, fell asleep in Jesus at Menton, January 31, 1892. I have fought a good fight, I have finished my course, I have kept the faith."

Indeed he did.

by Rod Thomson

*Rod Thomson is an award-winning journalist and writer in Sarasota, Florida, and the administrator of Hand to the Plow Ministries.*

# Illustration Portfolio

THE BIRTHPLACE OF CHARLES H. SPURGEON
June 19, 1834 in Kelvedon, Essex, England

REV. JOHN SPURGEON
father of C.H. Spurgeon

ELIZA SPURGEON
mother of C.H. Spurgeon

NEW PARK STREET CHAPEL

NEAR THIS SPOT ON 6TH JAN. 1950
PASTOR C.H. SPURGEON
FOUND PEACE THROUGH JESUS CHRIST AS DESCRIBED IN HIS OWN WORDS –
"SEEKING REST, AND FINDING NONE, I STEPPED WITHIN THE HOUSE OF GOD, AND SAT
THERE, AFRAID TO LOOK UPWARD, LEST I SHOULD BE UTTERLY CUT OFF, AND LEST HIS
FIERCE WRATH SHOULD CONSUME ME. THE MINISTER ROSE IN HIS PULPIT, AND READ
THIS TEXT, "LOOK UNTO ME, AND BE YE SAVED ALL THE ENDS OF THE EARTH, FOR I
AM GOD, AND THERE IS NONE ELSE."
I LOOKED THAT MOMENT: THE GRACE OF FAITH WAS VOUCHSAFED TO ME IN THAT
SELFSAME INSTANT; AND NOW I THINK I CAN SAY WITH TRUTH –
E'ER SINCE BY FAITH I SAW THE STREAM,
HIS FLOWING WOUNDS SUPPLY,
REDEEMING LOVE HAS BEEN MY THEME,
AND SHALL BE TILL I DIE."

———————

THIS TABLET WAS UNVEILED BY
SIR W.D. PEARSON, BART, M.P.
APRIL 16TH 1897.
IN THE SIXTIETH YEAR OF THE REIGN OF
HER MAJESTY QUEEN VICTORIA

*Above:* The cottage where Mr. Spurgeon preached his first sermon at age 16. *Left:* Susannah Tompson became Mrs. Charles Spurgeon on January 8, 1856. Despite fragile health, she was a strong partner to her husband and his ministry. *Below:* The Spurgeons lived a comfortable but modest life at Westwood, and used the majority of their income to help ministers, the poor, and people in need.

WESTWOOD

THE NEW PARK STREET CHAPEL
Spurgeon accepted his first pastorate in December 1853,
at the age of nineteen.

MUSIC HALL IN THE ROYAL SURREY GARDENS
In spite of a disasterous beginning, the congregation used this
building as a meeting place for five years.

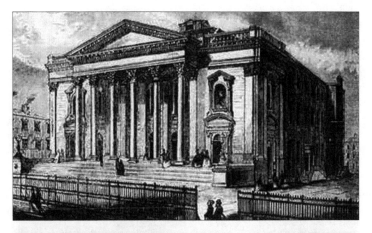

NEW PARK STREET CHAPEL.

THE METROPOLITAN TABERNACLE
*Above*: Completed in 1861, the new home of the Park Street congregation was built in the Greek style. It was the largest church in the world at the time and held nearly 6,000 people.
*Left*: Spurgeon sometimes needed to be helped into the pulpit because of the pain he suffered from gout.

STOCKWELL ORPHANAGE

Spurgeon oversaw and raised funds to support the Boy's School and Girl's School at Stockwell Orphanage (*above*), as well as the Pastor's College he founded (*bottom*).

THE PASTOR'S COLLEGE

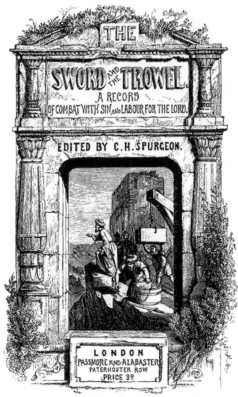

THE SWORD AND THE TROWEL
Spurgeon published this monthly magazine beginning in 1865, in which he essentially continued preaching Christ, but also touched on issues of doctrine within the church.

Spurgeon in his study at Westwood, his family home.

Spurgeon's study at Westwood (*above*) contained more than 12,000 volumes. Mr. Spurgeon's work was enormous.

Besides editing and furnishing most of the matter for his monthly magazine, *The Sword and Trowel*, since January 1, 1865, he wrote *The Saint and His Saviour, The Treasury of David, an Exposition of the Psalms* in seven octavo volumes; *The New Park Street Pulpit* and the *Metropolitan Tabernacle Pulpit*, which contains about two thousand of his weekly sermons from 1855 to 1889, making thirty large volumes. Also *Lectures to My Students, Commenting and Commentaries, John Ploughman*, the *Cheque Book of the Bank of Faith*, and various other publications.

Mark XVI. 14!

This shows us the way in wh we must deal with
unbelief in ourselves, & in others. It is a sin
& should be treated as such. Jesus wd not have
upbraided had not this been the case.
In the case before us they had repeated
testimonies, from their own brethren, & backed by
his own word — but we have even more
guilt for we know him to be risen & yet doubt

I. Let us consider its evil in itself
Suppose some one doubted us.
Think of who he is & what he has done.
Consider his near & dear relation to us.
The many times in wh we have doubted
And upon the same matter.
Where his promises forbade unbelief
Despite our own declarations.
What have we believed in preference?

II. Let us observe the evils wt it causes
It grieves the Spirit of God.
It causes distress in our own hearts
It weakens us for action or suffering
It depresses others.
It leaves an ill impres con sinners
It cannot but gender to bondage

III. Let us reflect upon its sinfulness where
it reigns
It gives God the lie.
It argues hatred in the heart
It is the sign of utter moral death.
It is the essence of hell.

SERMON NOTES
This one page of handwritten notes is all Spurgeon took with him
into the pulpit when he preached the sermon titled
"Unbelievers Upbraided."

# CHAPTER ONE

# A Personal Word to the Reader

All of Grace is written in child-like dependence on the Holy Spirit, and I trust He will use it to lead many to the Lord Jesus Christ. May the Lord visit you with His grace as you read the plain and simple words of this book. Whether you are rich or poor, well-educated or unlettered, I pray that you will read these words with understanding and that many who read will ultimately become great soul-winners.

Who knows how many people will find their way to peace by what they read in this book? More importantly, will *you* be one of them?

There once was a man who built a fountain along the wayside. Nearby, he attached a cup to a chain. After doing so, he heard that an art critic had found fault with the design of his fountain.

The man said, "But do many thirsty persons drink from it?"

Those who heard this question responded, "Thousands of men, women, and children get their thirst quenched at this fountain."

The man smiled and said, "Though I'm troubled by what the critic said, I hope he will come by on some sultry summer day, pick up the cup, fill it, drink from it, be refreshed, and praise the name of the Lord."

This book is a fountain from which you may drink the water of life. I've written if for *you*. I want it to bless your soul. So before you begin reading, be sure that your heart is open to God and His grace.

My goal in writing is that you would find Christ and know that you have a home in Heaven. As we proceed, therefore, let's seek Him together. Let's join our hearts in prayer, look up to God, and ask Him to bless you while you read.

It's not by accident that you are reading this book. Divine providence has led you to it. May God bless you while you read.

The Bible says, "Today, if ye will hear his voice, harden not your hearts" (Heb. 4:7).

# CHAPTER TWO

# A Gift from God

I once heard a story about a minister in northern England who called upon a very poor lady, intending to give financial help to her. With a monetary gift in hand, he knocked at her door, but there was no answer. He concluded that she was not at home, and so he left.

Later that evening, the minister saw the woman at church, and he told her that he had tried to visit her. He said, "I called at your house and knocked on your door several times, but there was no answer, so I assumed you were not at home."

She asked, "At what hour did you come by?"

"About noon."

"Oh, dear," she said, "I heard you, sir, and I am so sorry I did not come to the door, but I thought it was the landlord coming by for the rent money."

She was trying to avoid her landlord, because she was unable to pay the rent, and there are many people who know what that is like. In writing this book, however, I am not "calling for the rent." In fact, I'm not trying to make demands on you or ask anything from you.

## Salvation Is Free

All I want to do is to let you know that salvation is all by grace, which means it is absolutely *free*.

Too many people are like the woman I just mentioned when it comes to someone telling them about Jesus. They think, Oh, now I'm going to be told what my duty is. This person is going to try to get something from me, to collect what God wants from me, and I'm sure I don't have what He is looking for.

To the contrary, I did not write this book to get anything from you. Rather, *All of Grace* is written to bring something to you. In the pages of this book you will not find teaching about law, duty, and punishment; instead, you will learn about God's love, goodness, forgiveness, mercy, and His offer of eternal life.

So, as you read, don't pretend that you "are not at home," as the poor lady did. Do not turn a deaf ear or a careless heart to my words. I am asking nothing of you in the name of God or of man, and I have no desire to impose any requirements on you.

In writing this book I desire to bring you a free gift that will bring joy to you now and throughout all eternity. So open the door to your heart and receive what God has for you.

### Come Now

Isaiah wrote, "Come now, and let us reason together, saith the Lord: though your sins be as scarlet, they shall be as white as snow; though they be red like crimson, they shall be as wool" (Isa.1:18).

Here we see the Lord inviting you to a personal conference with Him. This meeting concerns your immediate and eternal happiness. You see, He wants the best for you, His child.

Therefore, I urge you not to refuse the Lord Jesus who is knocking at the door of your heart. Remember that He knocks with a hand that was nailed to the cross for you.

Your good is His object, so incline your ear to Him and let Him come in.

Jesus said, "Behold, I stand at the door, and knock: If any man hear my voice, and open the door, I will come in to him, and will sup with him, and he with me" (Rev.3:20).

Dear reader, hearken to His invitation, and let His good words sink into your soul. As you do so, your life will begin anew and you will be on your way to Heaven.

### Faith Comes by Hearing

Paul writes, "So then faith cometh by hearing, and hearing by the word of God" (Rom.10:17). Reading this book is like hearing; therefore, faith will come to you while you are reading this book.

My prayer for you is that the Holy Spirit will apply these truths to your heart and life. O blessed Spirit of all grace, make it so!

# CHAPTER THREE

# God Justifies the Ungodly

The message of this chapter is written for *you*. Let me begin by referring you to a verse that was written by the apostle Paul: "Now to him that worketh is the reward not reckoned of grace, but of debt. But to him that worketh not, but believeth on him that justifieth the ungodly, his faith is counted for righteousness" (Rom. 4:4-5).

I want to call your attention to these particular words of Scripture: "Him that justifieth the ungodly." These are very wonderful words, indeed, because they reveal that God has the power to regard and treat the ungodly as righteous and worthy of salvation when they come to Him by faith. (For more about the subject of justification, please refer to the glossary at the end of this book.)

I have heard some people say that they hate the doctrines of the cross, and many will even find fault with God because He saves wicked people and receives the vilest of the vile unto Himself.

The above verse confronts their charges with divine truth. Paul, by the inspiration of the Holy Spirit, reveals that God is pleased to justify the ungodly. In other words, He makes those *just* who are unjust, forgives those who deserve to be punished, and favors those who deserve no favor.

Perhaps you have thought that salvation was only for those who are good or that God's grace was for the pure and holy, those who are free from sin. It may well be that you have thought that if you could be excellent, God would reward you. In all likelihood, you have thought these things because you realize you are not worthy, and this has led you to believe that there could be no way for you to enjoy God's favor.

Therefore, you must be pleasantly surprised to read a verse from the Bible that tells you that God justifies the ungodly. I understand why you are surprised by this, because I never cease to be amazed by the great grace of God in our lives. It is surprising that a holy God would be able to justify unholy men and women.

People often tend to want to talk about their own goodness and worthiness, believing that there is something within them that will attract God's attention and favor. God, however, sees through all our self-deceptions, and He knows that there is no goodness at all within us.

This is confirmed by His words to the prophet Isaiah, who wrote, "But we are all as an unclean thing, and all our righteousnesses are as filthy rags" (Isa.64:6). Jesus came not because we are just; He came to make us just. Through Him God justifies the ungodly.

### Justifying the Guilty

When an honest attorney goes into court in behalf of an innocent person, he or she will plead the client's case before the court, making every effort to justify the client and find exoneration from all alleged crimes for that one. The lawyer's object is to justify the innocent person, but he or she should not attempt to justify someone who is guilty. Justifying the guilty is not a human right; this is a miracle that is reserved for the Lord alone.

God, the infinitely just Sovereign of the universe, knows that there is not a just person—someone who does only good and never sins—on the earth. Because this is true, in the infinite sovereignty of His divine nature and the splendor of His ineffable love, God undertakes the task of justifying the ungodly.

God has devised effective ways and means for making an ungodly person to be able to stand before Him as being justly accepted. He has set up a system whereby He can treat the guilty person with perfect justice, as if he or she had been wholly free from sin throughout his or her lifetime. This is what is meant by the phrase, "He justifies the ungodly."

We must remember that Jesus Christ came into the world to save sinners. (See 1 Tim.1:15.) This is a marvelous thing and something that should cause people to stand in awe of God. To know that God has justified even *me* truly is a marvel, and it's the greatest wonder I have ever known.

Why do I feel this way? It's because I would feel as if I am a lump of unworthiness, a mass of corruption, and a heap of sin if I did not know God's almighty love and wonderful grace in my life. But now I know with full assurance that I have been justified by faith in Christ Jesus, and I am treated by Him as if I had always been perfectly just. Now I know that I am an heir of God and a joint heir with Christ. Even though I am undeserving of God's grace, I am treated as though I am deserving of it, and I know I am loved with as much love as I would have received if I had always been godly. How could one help but be astonished by this? My gratitude for such divine favor stands dressed in robes of wonder.

### Good News for You!

Though these are surprising and wonderful truths, the point is that the Gospel of Jesus Christ—His good news—is available to you and me. God justifies the ungodly, and He can justify *you*. If you are unconverted, you are an ungodly person. If you have lived without God, you are an ungodly person. Perhaps you have disregarded God's day, God's house, and God's Word; if so, you are an ungodly person.

Sadder still, you may have tried to deny the existence of God even though you've lived on this beautiful earth, which is so full of tokens of God's presence and His creative power. If so, you are an ungodly person, and you have lived as if there is no God. If what I've said is true of you, I'm sure you would have been very pleased if you could have demonstrated to yourself that God does not exist.

If any of these things apply to you, it may well be that you have lived a great many years in ungodliness, so that now you are very well settled in your ways and God is not found in any of your ways. Therefore, the term "ungodly person" is an apt description of you in the same way that someone might label the sea simply as "salt water."

Possibly, however, you are different from the descriptions I've given above. It may well be that you have regularly attended to all the outward forms of religion, but your heart has not been in them. In this sense, therefore, you are an ungodly person. Though you've met with the people of God, you have not met with God himself. Perhaps you've sung in a church choir, but you have not praised the Lord with your heart.

It could be that you have not loved God with all your heart, and you have not obeyed Him. If any of these things apply to you, I want you to know that God justifies the ungodly. You can apply this truth to your life by faith.

When God justifies you, it will be as if you never sinned. Isn't that wonderful?

I pray that you will accept this good news into your heart and life. If you are a sensible person, you will see how God has provided His remarkable grace for your life, and you will cry, "God justifies the ungodly! Why, then, should I not be justified? I want to be justified now!"

God's great salvation is available to you even though you do not deserve it and have no preparation for it. If you cannot justify yourself, you need to experience God's justification. However, if you feel that you are perfectly righteous, you will feel that you do not need to be justified. You may even feel that you are doing your duty perfectly well as it is; hence, you will feel no need for God's justification in your life.

You may even think that Heaven has an obligation to you because you have been so "righteous." If this is true of you, you are unlikely to sense a need for the Savior or for divine mercy in any form. You could be thinking, Why do I need justification? If this is true of you, you are probably already tired of this book. There will be little from here on that will interest you.

## Self-Righteousness

Be careful, though, if this is the case with you, for such an attitude comes from pride. Please listen to me. God justifies the ungodly. You need His justification in your life. If you do not heed these words, you will die in your sins, and you will be lost, as sure as you are alive right now!

The Scriptures tell us that no one is righteous. Jesus Christ did not come to call the righteous, but He did come to save sinners. Therefore, I am not writing this book to call the righteous to salvation. I am calling the ungodly and the unrighteous to receive God's grace in their lives.

Without Christ, any righteousness you perceive in your life is a total delusion. It has no more substance than a cobweb. Get rid of all such self-delusions, and flee from their influence in your life. Understand that the only people who can be justified by God are those who do not attempt to justify themselves. Realize that you need God to make you just; He is the One who will enable you to stand before His judgment seat in the righteousness that only Christ can provide for you.

### The Lord Will Meet Your Needs

The Lord promises to meet your needs. In His infinite wisdom, He is not interested in providing you with anything that is unnecessary. Jesus does not concern himself with superfluous things. He has no interest in justifying someone who is already just before God. In His infinite love and mercy, He wants to justify the ungodly. This is a marvelous miracle of God.

A physician who has certain cures at his or her disposal goes forth to help those who are sick. He or she is not involved in reaching out to healthy people. If you were to put such a doctor in a locale where there were no sick people, he or she would certainly feel out of place, because there would be nothing for him or her to do.

Jesus said, "They that are whole have no need of the physician, but they that are sick: I came not to call the righteous, but sinners to repentance" (Mark 2:17). The great and effective remedies of grace and redemption are for those who are sick in soul—the ungodly—not for those who are whole.

The Great Physician, the Lord Jesus Christ, came into the world for you. Do you feel that you are spiritually sick? Are you altogether undone because of your sin? If your answer to either or both of these questions is "yes," you are ready to receive the benefits of God's grace, as they are outlined in His plan of salvation. The Lord looks upon you with love, and He wants you to receive His gift of grace.

Let's imagine that a very generous man decides to forgive the debts of all those who owe money to him. All he asks is for the debtors to come to him, so he can cancel their debts and write "paid in full" on their bills. This would truly be a very wonderful thing for the debtors; however, this generous man would not be able to forgive the debts of people who do not owe anything to him.

Similarly, God, who is omnipotent in His power to forgive sin, cannot forgive someone who is without sin, because forgiveness would not be needed in such a case. His pardon is for the guilty, not for the innocent. His forgiveness is for the sinful, not for the sinless.

Has it occurred to you that you are lost because you are a sinner? It is because you are a sinner that you can be saved. God's grace has been ordained for you. So pay attention to the lines of this hymn:

*A sinner is a sacred thing;*
*The Holy Spirit hath made him so.*

### Jesus Seeks and Saves the Lost

Jesus seeks and saves that which is lost. He died on the cross, and in so doing, He made atonement for sinners—those who recognize that they are sinners in need of God's mercy and grace. The inn of mercy never closes its doors on those who know their need before God.

Our Lord Jesus Christ did not die for imaginary sins, but His heart's blood was shed to cleanse the crimson stains of real sin. Nothing but His blood can wash away our sins.

I know of a preacher of the gospel who preached a sermon that was built from this text: "And now also the axe is laid unto the root of the trees: every tree therefore which bringeth not forth good fruit is hewn down, and cast into the fire" (Luke 3:9).

After hearing his sermon, a member of the congregation commented, "One would have thought that you were preaching to criminals!"

The preacher responded, "Oh, no, if I were preaching in the county jail, I should not preach from that text, for there I would preach, 'This is a faithful saying, and worthy of all acceptation, that Christ Jesus came into the world to save sinners.'"

The minister was exactly right. The Law is for the self-righteous, and it brings with it humility to take away their pride. The Gospel of Jesus Christ, on the other hand, is for the lost, and it removes their despair.

If you are not lost, you no longer need to seek salvation from your sins. Would a shepherd go after sheep that had not gone astray? Why should a woman sweep her house to look for coins that never fell out of her purse? Medicine is for those who are sick, and quickening is for those who are dead. Similarly, pardon is for the guilty, liberation is for those who are bound, and the opening of eyes is for those who are blind.

The Savior's death upon the cross and His gospel of pardon are for those who are guilty of sin and worthy of condemnation. The gospel exists for sinners. Therefore, if you are undeserving, ill-deserving, and hell-deserving, you are the type of person for whom the Gospel of Jesus Christ was ordained. There is great hope for you, because God justifies the ungodly.

I want to make this vital message as clear and plain as possible. As I do so, however, I realize that only the Lord can make you actually see it. If your spirit is starting to awaken, you may be amazed that salvation has been provided for you—a lost and guilty soul. You might think, "Oh, but I must first be this or that." This is jumping ahead of yourself, for the things you want to be and should be will take place after salvation, but salvation must come to you first.

The grace of God reaches you when you are ungodly, and the Gospel of Jesus Christ comes to justify you. If you feel unworthy and think there is nothing good about you, reach out to God in faith. Believe that He is able and willing to take you as you are and to spontaneously forgive you. He doesn't do this because you are good, but only because *He* is good.

Jesus said, "He maketh His sun to rise on the evil and on the good, and sendeth rain on the just and on the unjust" (Matt.5:45). Does God not send the rain and the sunshine and give fruitful harvests to the most ungodly nations as well as to those that honor Him? Even Sodom experienced sunshine, and Gomorrah was watered with dew.

Oh, friend, God's great grace surpasses our understanding and comprehension. The Bible says, "Let the wicked forsake his way, and the unrighteous man his thoughts: and let him return unto the LORD, and he will have mercy upon him; and to our God, for he will abundantly pardon. For my thoughts are not your thoughts, neither are your ways my ways, saith the LORD. For as the heavens are higher than the earth, so are my ways higher than your ways, and my thoughts than your thoughts'" (Isa.55:7-8).

God is able to pardon you abundantly. Jesus Christ came into the world to save sinners. God's forgiveness is for those who are guilty.

### Jesus Will Receive You Just as You Are

Don't try to make yourself presentable to the Lord, and don't attempt to make yourself into something other than what you are. Come to Him as an ungodly person in need of a Savior, to the One who justifies the ungodly.

There was a great artist who painted a scene from a city in which he lived. For historical purposes he wanted to include certain characters in the painting that were well known in his town. One of these figures was a ragged and unkempt street sweeper who was well known to everyone who lived there. The artist approached him and said, "I will pay you well if you will come down to my studio and let me paint you." The man agreed, so he went to the artist's studio the next morning.

The artist had to send him away, however, because the man had washed his face, combed his hair, and put on respectable clothing. The artist wanted to paint a poor, unkempt man, not a clean and well-groomed man.

This is a good illustration of what I'm trying to convey in this chapter. The Lord Jesus will receive you just as you are, but you have to come as a sinner, not with any kind of self-righteousness. God justifies the *ungodly*, and the gospel meets you in your lowest estate.

So come to your heavenly Father in all your sin and sinfulness. Come to Jesus just as you are—leprous, filthy, naked, and unfit for either life or death. Come, even though you may feel you dare not hope for anything but death. Come, even though despair is brooding over you and you feel it pressing upon you like a horrible nightmare.

Come, and ask the Lord Jesus to justify you. Come for the great mercy of God, which is meant for you.

The Lord has taken this title upon Himself: "Him that justifieth the ungodly." He will make you *just*, even though you are ungodly by nature. Isn't this a wonderful message for you to consider? Do not delay. Receive God's grace and be justified.

# CHAPTER FOUR

# It Is God Who Justifies

The Bible says, "Who shall lay any thing to the charge of God's elect? It is God that justifieth" (Rom.8:33).

As we pointed out in the preceding chapter, God justifies the ungodly. One of the most important points to realize about this is that it is only God who can bring justification to you.

Justification is such a wonderful thing. If we had not broken God's laws, we would not need to be justified, because we would have been just in and of ourselves. No one is without sin; therefore, we all need to be justified.

You are deceiving yourself if you attempt to justify yourself, so don't even attempt to do so, for you will surely fail. By the same token, don't ask others to justify you, for they have no power to do so. The best you can expect from others is that they might speak well of you. However, they might also gossip about you. The important thing to realize is that their opinions and judgments are not worth much.

It is God who justifies. This is an astonishing fact, one that you need to consider with care.

When you think about it, you realize that no one but God would have ever thought of justifying those who are guilty. He is willing to justify even those who have lived in open rebellion toward Him, and those who have done evil with their hands. God justifies those who have returned to sin, those who have broken the Law, and those who have trampled on the gospel.

God justifies those who have refused His proclamations of mercy, and persist in their ungodliness. How can these people be forgiven and justified? Others might say, "They are hopeless cases!" Even Christians may look upon them with sorrow and pity rather than hope.

### The Light of the Gospel

God, however, views them in a different light—the light of the Gospel of Jesus Christ. In the splendor of His grace, He chose them from the foundation of the world, and He will not rest until they receive the justification He has provided for them and until they are accepted in the Beloved. (See Eph.1:6.)

Paul writes, "Moreover whom he did predestinate, them he also called: whom he called, them he also justified: and whom he justified, them he also glorified" (Rom.8:30).

This passage reveals that the Lord resolves to justify certain people, and why shouldn't you be one of those He has predestined and called to be justified and glorified?

I can assure you that no one but God would have ever thought of justifying *me*. This is a wonder even to me. Look at Saul of Tarsus, who foamed at the mouth as he ranted and raged against God's servants. Like a hungry wolf, he brought fear to the lambs and the sheep within the Good Shepherd's fold. Despite his actions, God struck Saul down on the road to Damascus, and completely changed his heart.

God justified Saul, and, as Paul the apostle, he became the greatest preacher of justification by faith that ever lived. I can well imagine that he must have often marveled over the fact that he was justified by faith in Christ Jesus, for he had once been a stickler for salvation through the works of the Law. No one but God would have ever thought of justifying Saul the persecutor. He did so because He is glorious in grace.

Even if someone else would think about justifying someone who is ungodly, only God himself could accomplish this great miracle. It is quite impossible for a person to forgive offenses that have not been committed against him or her. If someone greatly injures you in some way, it is possible for you to forgive them, and I hope you will, but no one else can forgive that person for you. If the wrong is done to you, the pardon must come from you.

Likewise, if we have sinned against God, it is in God's power to forgive us, for the sin is against Him. This is what David meant when he prayed, "Against thee, thee only, have I sinned, and done this evil in thy sight" (Ps.51:4).

David accurately recognized that he had committed offenses against God, and he knew that only God could forgive him for those offenses. God can remit our sins, and when He does so, they are completely gone! He has the power to blot out all of our sins. For this reason we must go to Him and seek His mercy.

### *The One Mediator between God and Us*

Don't be led astray by anyone who would urge you to confess your sins to him or her. The Word of God is clear about this; only God, not another human being, can justify you. Paul writes, "For there is one God, and one mediator between God and men, the man Christ Jesus" (1 Tim.2:5).

The Lord Jesus Christ is the Mediator between you and God, and through Him alone you are able to find pardon for your sins.

Yes, only God can justify the ungodly, and He does so with perfection. He casts our sins behind His back. He blots them out. He says that they cannot be found even if we try to search for them. Out of His infinite goodness and grace, He has prepared a glorious way by which He can make our scarlet sins as white as snow. (See Isa.1:18.) He wants to remove your transgressions from you as far as the east is from the west. (See Ps.103:12.) He says to you, "I will not remember your sins."

The prophet Micah writes, "Who is a God like unto thee, that pardoneth iniquity, and passeth by the transgression of the remnant of his heritage?" (Mic.7:18).

We are not dealing here with justice or with God giving people what they deserve. If you try to deal with the righteous Lord according to the Law, everlasting wrath will threaten you, for that is what you deserve. Blessed be His name, God has not dealt with us according to our sins; but He comes to us with free grace and infinite compassion.

He says, "I will receive you graciously, and I will love you freely." Believe this, for it is completely true. Through Christ, our great God is able to extend His wonderful mercy to the guilty and to treat the ungodly as if they had always been godly.

### The Prodigal Son

Take a few moments now to carefully read the Parable of the Prodigal Son. (See Luke 15.) Notice how the forgiving father in this story receives his returning son with great love, as if he had never defiled himself with harlots and loose living. He receives his son as if he had never left home in the first place.

The elder brother becomes envious regarding his father's treatment of his brother, but the father never withdraws his love for the Prodigal Son or his brother. God, our heavenly Father, treats us in the same way. No matter how guilty you may be, if you will only come back to your God and Father, He will treat you as if you have never done anything wrong! He will see you as a just person, and He will deal with you accordingly.

Like the Prodigal Son, will you return to your true Father and receive His love and blessings? This is a choice you will never regret.

It is all so splendid and amazing. None but God would think of justifying the ungodly, and none but God could accomplish this great miracle in a sinner's life. When God justifies a person, it is well done, rightly done, justly done, and everlasting done.

### The Riches of God's Mercy

I read an article in a magazine that was full of venom against the gospel and those who preach it. The writer said that we have some kind of "theory" through which we imagine that sin can be removed from a person's life. Obviously, this writer does not understand the Gospel of Jesus Christ. We hold to no particular theory; instead, we preach glorious facts, and the greatest of all facts is this – that Christ by His precious blood actually does put away sin, and that God, for Christ's sake, deals with people according to His divine mercy, forgiving and justifying the guilty. These things are not accomplished through anything that God sees or foresees in human beings, but they take place according to the riches of His mercy, which lie deep within His heart.

This is what I have preached, continue to preach, and will preach as long as I live. It is God who justifies the ungodly, and He is not ashamed of doing so, and I am not ashamed of preaching about it.

The justification that comes from God is beyond all questioning. If the Judge acquits me, who can condemn me?

If the highest court in the universe has pronounced me to be just, who shall be able to register anything against me?

Justification from God is a sufficient answer for a person's awakened conscience. When we are justified, the Holy Spirit breathes peace over our entire nature, and we are no longer afraid. Through justification we can answer all the roars and railings of Satan and ungodly people. It enables us to face death, because justification helps us to know that we shall rise again.

> *Bold shall I stand in that great day,*
> *For who aught to my charges shall lay?*
> *While by my Lord absolved I am*
> *From sin's tremendous curse and blame.*
> (Count Nicolaus Ludwig Zinzendorf, 1700-1760)

Dear reader, the Lord can blot out *all your sins*. It is no "shot in the dark" when I say, "God forgives all manner of sin." Even if you are up to your neck in crime and sin, God can remove it with a single word, and He will say, *"Be clean. This is My will for you."* The Lord is the Great Forgiver.

I believe in the forgiveness of sins. Do you? At this very moment the Lord could say to you, *"Your sins are forgiven. Go in peace."* When this happens, there will be no power on earth or under the earth that will be able to put you under suspicion or wrath. So don't doubt the power of God's almighty love.

If another person offended you in the way that you have offended God, you would find it most difficult, if not impossible, to forgive that one. God's ways are far different from human ways, so don't measure Him by your own standards. God's thoughts and ways are far above your thoughts and ways, as the heavens are high above the earth.

"Well," you might say, "it would be a great miracle if the Lord were to pardon me." Indeed, it would be a supreme miracle, and He is likely to accomplish that miracle because He wants to do so and is able to do so. God always does great and unsearchable things for those He loves.

There was a time in my life when I was burdened with a horrible sense of guilt, which made my life a complete misery, but God spoke to me and everything changed. He said, *"Look unto me, and be ye saved, all the ends of the earth: for I am God, and there is none else."* (See Isa.45:22.)

I responded to His command with obedience. I looked unto Him, and in a single moment the Lord justified me. It was then that I saw that Jesus Christ, who knew no sin, had been made sin for me! (See 2 Cor.5:21.) That glimpse of Him gave me the most wonderful and complete rest I'd ever known.

When those who were bitten by the fiery serpents in the wilderness looked to the serpent of brass, they were healed at once; and I was spiritually healed when I looked to the crucified Savior. The Holy Spirit, who enabled me to believe, gave me peace through believing. I felt certain that I had been forgiven and cleansed, whereas before I had felt only condemnation and uncertainty.

Before this wonderful transformation occurred in my life, I felt certain of my condemnation, which the Word of God declared and my conscience confirmed. When the Lord justified me, however, the Word of God and my conscience gave me a different message—one of peace, mercy, love, and justification.

The Bible says, "He that believeth on him is not condemned: but he that believeth not is condemned already, because he hath not believed in the name of the only begotten Son of God" (John 3:18). My conscience assured me that I had truly believed in Jesus and His name, and I realized that the God who pardoned me was completely just.

I had the witness of the Holy Spirit and the witness of my own conscience, and these two agreed as one. These two witnesses made me know that I had been fully justified by God.

Oh, how I wish that you would receive God's testimony with regard to this vital matter. When you do so, you will have the inner witness that I've just described.

A sinner who is justified by God stands on a more solid and sure foundation than those who think they are justified by their own works. Such persons can never be sure that they have done enough works to become acceptable unto God. This, I'm sure, would lead them to have a very uneasy conscience, a fear of always falling short before God and receiving His punishment for so doing.

When God justifies a person and the Holy Spirit bears witness to that justification, that person enters into peace with God. This is a most desirable place—to realize that the matter of justification is sure and settled, and that we have entered into God's rest. (See Heb. 4.) It is impossible to adequately describe the deep sense of calm which comes over the soul that has received God's wonderful peace, which surpasses all understanding. (See Phil.4:6-7.)

This peace and rest can be yours today!

# CHAPTER FIVE

# How Can a Just God Justify the Guilty?

In the preceding chapters we have seen that it is God who justifies the ungodly, and we have seen that He is the only one who can do so. In this chapter we will answer the question: How can a just God justify the guilty?

Paul gives us a direct answer to this question: "But now the righteousness of God without the law is manifested, being witnessed by the law and the prophets; even the righteousness of God which is by faith of Jesus Christ unto all and upon all them that believe: for there is no difference: for all have sinned, and come short of the glory of God; being justified freely by his grace through the redemption that is in Christ Jesus: whom God hath set forth to be a propitiation through faith in his blood, to declare his righteousness for the remission of sins that are past, through the forbearance of God; to declare, I say, at this time his righteousness: that he might be just, and the justifier of him which believeth in Jesus" (Rom.3:21-26).

## The Justice of God

When I was under the hand of the Holy Spirit, under the conviction of sin, I had a clear and sharp sense of the justice of God. Sin, whatever it might be to other people, became an intolerable burden to me. It was not so much that I feared hell, but that I feared sin. I knew myself to be so horribly guilty that I remember feeling that if God did not punish me for sin, He ought to do so.

I truly felt that the Judge of all the Earth ought to condemn such sins as mine. I sat on the judgment seat, and I condemned myself to perish. I confessed that if I had been God, I could have done nothing else than send such a guilty creature as me to the lowest hell! All the while, I had a deep concern for the honor of God's name and the integrity of His moral government. I felt that it would not satisfy my conscience if I were to be forgiven unjustly. I reasoned that I had to be punished for the sin I had committed.

I wrestled with the question, How can a just God justify the guilty? On a more personal level I asked, How can God justify me, for I am so guilty? How can He be both the Just and the Justifier? These questions worried and wearied me, and I could not come up with a reasonable answer to either of them. Certainly I couldn't invent any answer that would truly satisfy my conscience.

### The Doctrine of the Atonement and the Plan of Salvation

The doctrine of the Atonement is one of the surest proofs for the divine inspiration of the Holy Scriptures. Who could have or would have thought of the Just Ruler dying for unjust rebels? This is neither mythology nor poetry, and no fiction devised by mankind would ever propose such a seemingly far-fetched idea. This wonderful plan was not devised by human beings; God is the One who ordained it.

I had heard about the plan of salvation and the sacrifice of Jesus from the early days of my youth, but I did not know about it personally within my innermost being. The light was there, but I was blind to it. The Lord had to make the matter plain to me.

When He did so, it came to me as a new revelation—a revelation that Jesus Christ was the propitiation for *my* sins and a revelation that God was just. I believe the substitutionary sacrifice of Jesus must come as a revelation to each person who needs to be saved.

I came to understand that Jesus' death on the cross made it possible for me to be saved. God had made provision for His sacrificial death—a vicarious sacrifice for the ungodly. I was made to see that Jesus, the Son of God, the One who is co-equal and co-eternal with the Father, established a New Covenant with God's people. He became the Covenant-Head of God's chosen ones, so that He might suffer for them and save them.

As a result of the fall of Adam, we became a fallen people. Therefore, we needed the last Adam (Christ) to deliver us and recover us from the Fall. I began to see that before I had ever sinned, I was a sinner because of Adam's sin. Then I began to rejoice, when I realized that Jesus made it possible for me to escape from the fallen condition in which I found myself.

Adam's fall had left a loophole through which I could escape. The last Adam was able to undo the ruin that was caused by the first Adam. As I wrestled with my guilt and my feeling that a just God would punish me for my sin, I began to see that Jesus Christ was the Son of God who became a man. I then realized that He died for me on Calvary's cross. He bore my sin in His own blessed person —His own blessed body—on the tree.

I realized that the chastisement of my peace had been laid on Him and that with His stripes I was healed. (See Isa.53:5.)

Dear reader, have you ever seen these things about Jesus? Have you ever understood how God can be fully just and not remit the penalties nor blunt the edge of His sword, and yet He can also be infinitely merciful and can justify the ungodly who turn to Him in faith?

### The Death of Jesus

It was because the Son of God, Who is supremely glorious in His matchless person, undertook to vindicate the Law by bearing the sentence that was due to me that God is able to remit my sin. The Law of God was more vindicated by the death of Christ than it would have been had all transgressors been sent to hell. That the Son of God suffered for sin was a glorious establishment of the government of God, a more glorious establishment of His government than could have ever taken place if the whole race had to suffer.

Jesus has borne the death penalty in our behalf. Behold the wonder surrounding the death of Jesus on the tree. The greatest sight you will ever see is Jesus hanging on the cross. The Son of God (also known as the Son of man) was nailed to the cross and had to bear unimaginable pain for the unjust. The Just died for the unjust in order to bring us to God.

Oh, the glory of that scene. The Innocent One was punished in our stead. The Holy One was condemned! The Ever-Blessed One was made a curse for us! The infinitely glorious One was put to a shameful death!

The more I contemplate the suffering that Jesus went through in our behalf, the more certain I am that those sufferings were sufficient to deal with my sin. He suffered in order to take sin's penalty away from us. He turned it aside by His death. It is completely turned aside, and because this is true, those who believe in Jesus do not need to fear death any longer.

The foundation of God's throne is not shaken by this glorious truth. God's wrath toward sin and iniquity must be more terrible than we can imagine. Moses asked him, "Who knows the power of your anger?" As He yielded up His spirit, Jesus cried, "My God, my God, why hast thou forsaken me?" (Mark 15:34). These words help us to understand that God's justice was satisfied by Jesus' perfect obedience and terrible death. God was bowing before His own law.

Jesus' loving sacrifice makes it possible for all our sins to be swallowed up. His death on the cross makes it possible for God to look upon us with favor even though we are unworthy of His favor. That the Lord Jesus Christ took our place is the miracle of all miracles. He stood in our stead, and He bore our sins, as the following stanza proclaims:

> *Bear that we might never bear*
> *His Father's righteous ire.*

Jesus said, "It is finished" (John 19:30). The debt was paid, and this is what makes it possible for the unjust to be justified. God will spare the sinner because He did not spare His own Son. God can pass by your transgressions because He laid them upon His only begotten Son 2,000 years ago. If you believe in Jesus, you can be sure that your sins were carried away by Him, because He became the scapegoat for His people.

### What Does Believing in Jesus Entail?

Believing in Jesus involves far more than just saying, "He is God, and He is Savior." To believe in Jesus is to trust Him wholly and entirely and to take Him as your Savior, Lord, and Master from this time forth and forevermore.

Will you have Jesus? Will you take Him as your Savior? Remember, He already has you.

If you believe in Him, you cannot go to hell, for going to hell would make His sacrifice ineffectual. Jesus' sacrifice was accepted by God to provide remission for our sins. You do not have to die spiritually because Jesus has died for you; He died in your place.

You need to understand that He died for *you*. His sacrifice was made for *you*. By faith you can lay your hands upon it and make it your own. When you do so, you can know for sure that you will never perish.

God would not receive Jesus' sacrifice on our behalf and then condemn us to die. The Lord will not read our pardon, which was written with Jesus' blood, and then smite us. I pray that God will give you the grace to look to Jesus and start your life anew. Jesus is the fountainhead of mercy to the guilty!

Yes, God justifies the ungodly and He is the only one who can do so. Therefore, you can be justified through the atoning sacrifice of His divine Son, the Lord Jesus Christ. And it can be justly done—so justly done that no one will question it. It will be done thoroughly, as well— so thoroughly that in the final days, when Heaven and earth will pass away, no one shall be able to deny the validity of justification in the believer's life.

Will you come into the lifeboat of God's grace just as you are? God wants you to be safe and secure. Accept His sure deliverance. You might say, "I don't have anything to bring with me." That's all right; you do not have to bring anything with you. A person who is escaping from a horrible situation in order to save his or her life is not concerned about possessions. In fact, the person might possibly leave his or her possessions, including even clothing, behind. So take the leap of faith just as you are.

My sole hope for Heaven lies in the full atonement that Jesus made for the ungodly on Calvary's cross. I firmly rely on this truth. I do not see even the shadow of hope in anything else, anyone else, or anywhere else.

You and I are in the same condition. We have nothing in and of ourselves on which we can rely. Therefore, let's join hands and stand together at the foot of the cross. Let's entrust our souls to Jesus, who shed His blood for the guilty.

He loves you, and He will save you.

# CHAPTER SIX

# *Deliverance from Sinning*

Now it is time to say a few words to those who understand justification by faith in Christ Jesus but continue to struggle with sin in their lives. At the outset, let me say that you can never be truly happy, restful, or spiritually healthy until you have become holy.

How can we rid ourselves of sin? The old nature is very strong, and you may have tried to curb and tame it, but you have found that it will not be subdued. You may feel that you cannot cease from sin and, though you are anxious to do better, you find that things are getting worse instead of better.

Does this describe you? Your heart is so hard, your will is so obstinate, your passions are so furious, your thoughts are so volatile, your imagination is so ungovernable, and your desires are so wild that you feel you have a den of wild beasts within you, which are ready to devour you if you try to rule over them.

We may say of our fallen nature what the Lord said to Job concerning Leviathan: "Wilt thou play with him as with a bird? Or wilt thou bind him for thy maidens?" (Job 41:5). A man might as well hope to hold the north wind in the hollow of his hand as to expect to control by his own strength the boisterous powers that dwell within his fallen nature! This is a greater feat than any of the fabled labors of Hercules!

We need God to help us. A person might say, I could believe that Jesus would forgive sin, but then my trouble is that I sin again and that I feel such awful tendencies toward evil within me. I have an analogy that helps to explain this phenomenon. In the same way that a stone if tossed into the air returns to the ground, a person who is lifted by earnest preaching will eventually return to his or her sin. This happens because we are enticed by the eyes of sin, which holds us under a spell, and this keeps us from being able to escape on our own.

### Sanctification

Dear reader, I want you to know that salvation would be a sadly incomplete affair if it did not deal with deliverance from sin. We want to be purified as well as pardoned. Justification without sanctification would not truly be salvation. It would be like someone saying to a leper that he or she is clean, and then leaving him or her to die from the disease! Such a salvation would forgive the rebellion and then allow the rebel to remain an enemy of his or her king. It would remove the consequences while overlooking the causes, and this would leave us with endless and hopeless difficulties.

Such a salvation would stop the stream for a time, but leave an open fountain of defilement, which would sooner of later break forth with ever-increasing power. Remember that the Lord Jesus came to take away sin in three ways: He came to remove the *penalty* of sin, the *power* of sin, and the *presence* of sin from our lives.

When the power of sin is broken in your life, you will be ready to move on to the complete removal of all presence of sin in your life. The Bible says, "And ye know that he was manifested to take away our sins; and in him is no sin" (1 John 3:5).

The angel said of the Lord, "... thou shalt call his name JESUS: for he shall save his people from their sins" (Matt.1:21). Our Lord Jesus came to destroy the works of the devil within us. That which was said at our Lord's birth was also declared in His death, for when the soldier pierced His side, blood and water flowed out. This speaks of the double cure, by which we are delivered from the guilt and defilement of sin.

### A Change of Heart

If you are troubled by the power of sin in your life and the tendencies of your nature, I have a biblical promise for you. Put your faith in it and stand upon it, for it stems from the covenant of grace God has established for us. God, who cannot lie, said, "A new heart also will I give you, and a new spirit will I put within you: and I will take away the stony heart out of your flesh, and I will give you an heart of flesh" (Ezek.36:26).

You see, God is promising a new heart and a new spirit to you. He says, "I will," "I will give you," and "I will take away." These are the words of the King of kings, the Sovereign who is able to accomplish His will in your life. No word of His shall ever return to Him void. (See Isa.55:11.) His words shall never fall to the ground.

The Lord knows that you cannot change your own heart, and He knows that you cannot cleanse your own nature. He also knows that He can do both of these things for you. He can even cause a leopard to change its spots. He can create you anew. He can cause you to be born again. This transformation is a work of His grace—a true miracle—and it is accomplished through the power of the Holy Spirit.

35

It would be a wonderful thing to stand at the foot of Niagara Falls and speak a word that would make the Niagara River reverse its course and run upstream so you could watch the water leap over the great precipice over which it now rolls so forcefully. Only God could perform such a miracle, and He is able to reverse the course of your own nature. He is able to change the direction of your life.

Don't ever forget that *all* things are possible with God. He can reverse the direction of your desires and the whole current of your life. Instead of going downward from God, He can make your whole being turn upward toward Him. That is, in fact, what the Lord has promised to do for all who are recipients of His New Covenant. He will give you a new spirit and a new heart.

### God's Promises

Aren't these wonderful truths to think about? All the promises of God are yes and amen through Christ Jesus. (See 2 Cor. 1:20.) Take hold of His promises. Stand upon them. Accept them as truth. Appropriate them by faith for your own life. They are for you. Then begin to sing of the wonderful changes that God will bring to pass in your life.

When the Lord says He will take away our stony hearts, He means it, He does it, and we can know that He has done so. When He does this for us, no power can ever take your new heart and your right spirit away from you. The Bible says, "For the gifts and calling of God are without repentance" (Rom.11:29). God never takes away what He has given to us. Never!

So let Him renew you. You can be sure that He will do so. All your efforts at self-reformation and cleaning up your life are worthless, but when God puts a new heart within you, it remains forever, and it will never harden into stone again. He who transforms your heart from stone to flesh will keep it so.

### The Cat and the Sow

There is a wonderful illustration about a cat and a sow that was provided by a Mr. Rowland Hill. It helps us to understand this command of the Lord, "Ye must be born again" (John 3:7).

The cat is a very clean creature. She cleverly washes herself with her tongue and her paws, but did you ever see a sow do the same? No, it is contrary to the sow's nature to keep herself clean. She prefers to wallow in the mud and mire. If you were to try to teach a sow to wash herself, you would not be successful, for she would certainly return to the mire.

You may wash a sow by force, but it is still a useless task, because she will soon return to her preferred environment. The only way you would be able to teach a sow to wash herself would be to change her into a cat. Then she would endeavor to stay clean. Suppose you succeeded in bringing such a transformation to pass. The sow would then be fit for your parlor and your hearth rug.

It is the same way with an ungodly person. You cannot force an ungodly person to do what a renewed person does most willingly. You may teach such a one and set a good example for them, but an ungodly person cannot learn the art of holiness in these ways. Such a person wouldn't even want to learn it and would have no capacity to do so even if they did want it. The nature of the ungodly leads them in a direction that is completely different from holiness.

When the Lord makes someone new, however, everything changes. I once heard a new convert say, "Either all the world is changed or else I am!" The change that takes place when one is born again is tremendous. The new nature follows after right and good things as naturally as the old nature wandered after wrong things. What a blessing this is! God gives us a whole new nature! Only the Holy Spirit is able to accomplish such a miracle.

## A New Nature

What a wonderful thing it is for the Lord to give a person an entirely new nature. Have you ever seen a lobster that has lost one of its claws because it was in a fight with another lobster? Eventually the lobster grows a new claw where the old one had been. This is a truly remarkable aspect of nature, but it is even more remarkable to realize that God can actually give a new heart to a person who comes to Him by faith. This is a miracle that supersedes the powers of nature.

Think of a tree. If you cut off one of its limbs, another may grow in its place, but can you change the nature of the tree? Can you sweeten its sour sap? Can you make the thorn bear figs? You might be able to graft something new and better into the tree, but you cannot change its essence into another kind of tree. However, God in His great love for us, changes us completely when we place our faith and trust in Jesus.

If you will yield yourself to His divine working, the Lord will change your very nature. He will subdue your old nature and breathe new life into you. So put your trust in the Lord Jesus Christ, and He will take the stony heart out of your flesh and replace it with a heart of flesh.

The things about you that used to be hard will be tenderized. The things that used to be vicious will become virtuous. The good things in your life that were headed in a downward spiral will rise upward with powerful force. The lion of anger will give place to the lamb of meekness; the raven of uncleanness shall fly away before the dove of purity; and the vile serpent of deceit shall be trodden under the heel of truth.

With my own eyes I've seen radical changes in people's lives so that I am certain that no one is beyond God's reach. Previously unchaste women are now as pure as the driven snow. Men who used to be blasphemers now delight everyone around them by their intense devotion to the Lord. Thieves have been made honest, drunkards have been made sober, liars have become truthful, and scoffers have become zealous followers of the Lord.

When the grace of God reaches into the heart of a person, it trains that one to deny ungodliness and worldly lusts, to live soberly, righteously, and godly in this present evil world. (See Titus 2:12.) Dear reader, His grace will do the same for you!

I can imagine that some of you might say, "I cannot make this change." No one said you could. The Scriptures tell you what God will do for you, not what you can do for yourself. God will fulfill His promises to you. Trust in Him to bring His Word to pass in your life, and it will be done.

You might respond to this with the question, "But how is it to be done?" This truly is not your business. Must the Lord explain His methods to you before you will believe Him? Many aspects of the Lord's working in this matter remain within the realm of mystery. The Holy Spirit performs these supernatural miracles. The One who made the promise of new life has the responsibility of keeping the promise, and He is equal to that challenge!

God, who promises this marvelous change to you, will assuredly carry it out in your life when you receive Jesus as your Savior. When you do this, He will give you the power to become a child of God. (See John 1:12.)

Oh, that you would believe these truths. Trust the Lord to accomplish these miracles in your life. God cannot lie! So trust Him for a new heart and a right spirit to be imparted to you. He will give them to you! May the Lord give you faith in His promise, faith in His Son, faith in the Holy Spirit, and faith in Him. To Him be all glory, praise, and honor forever and ever! Amen!

# CHAPTER SEVEN

# *It Is by Grace through Faith*

Paul writes, "For by grace are ye saved though faith" (Eph.2:8). The fountainhead of our salvation is the grace of God. You are saved by grace. Because God is gracious He is able to forgive, convert, purify, and save sinful people. This does not happen because of anything they possess within themselves; it happens because of the boundless love, goodness, pity, compassion, mercy, and grace of God.

The grace of God is unlimited. Who can measure its breadth? Who can fathom its depths? Like all the other divine attributes, God's grace is infinite. He is full of love, for He is love. (See 1 John 4:8.) God is full of goodness; in fact, the very word *God* is short for "good." Unbounded goodness and love are found within the very essence of the Godhead. Because God's mercy endures forever, humanity has not been destroyed. Because His compassions do not fail, sinners come to Him and receive His forgiveness. (See Ps.136 and Lam.3:22.)

Be careful that you don't fall into error by fixing your mind so much upon faith—which is the channel of salvation—that you forget God's grace, which is the fountain and source of even faith itself. Remember that. Faith is the work of God's grace within us. No person can say that Jesus is the Christ except by the Holy Spirit. Jesus said, "No man can come to me, except the Father which hath sent me draw him" (John 6:44).

Therefore, the faith which leads us to Christ is imparted to us as the Father draws us to Him. Grace is the cause of salvation, and faith, as essential as it is, is only an important part of the machinery which grace employs. We are saved "through faith," but salvation is "by grace." Remember these words: "By grace you have been saved."

### *Faith Is the Channel*

Faith works like a channel or a conduit, but grace is the fountain and the stream. Faith is the aqueduct through which God's flood of mercy flows to refresh thirsty souls. It is a great pity when that aqueduct is broken. In the ruins of ancient Rome we see many noble aqueducts, which are no longer able to convey water into the city. It is sad to see such structures lying in ruin, unable to serve the purposes for which they were created. In order for an aqueduct to work properly, it must be maintained well. Likewise, faith must be true and sound, for it is the channel that leads us to God and brings mercy to our souls.

Let me reemphasize, though, that faith is only the channel or the aqueduct through which God's grace flows. It is not the source. It is not the fountainhead. The source of all divine blessings is found in the grace of God. Never make an idol of your faith, and don't ever make the mistake of thinking that faith is the independent source of your salvation.

New life is found by looking to Jesus, not in looking to your own faith. By faith all things become possible to us, but the power is not in the faith; it is in the God upon whom faith relies. Grace is the powerful engine, and faith is the chain by which the carriage of the soul is attached to its great source of power. The righteousness of faith

is not the moral excellence of faith, which is found in the righteousness of Jesus Christ, which grasps faith and appropriates it to our lives.

Peace within our souls is not derived from the contemplation of our own faith, but comes to us from Him who is our peace; and when our faith touches the hem of His garment, His power flows into our souls.

In light of all this, it is important for you to understand that the weakness of your faith will not destroy you. Even though a hand may be trembling, it can still receive a golden gift. The Lord's salvation can come to us even if we have faith the size of a mustard seed. The power is found in the grace of God, not in our faith.

Great messages can be sent through slender wires, and the peace-giving witness of the Holy Spirit can reach our hearts through thread-like faith, which seems very weak indeed. Look to the Lord, and see nothing but Jesus and God's grace that was revealed through Him.

# CHAPTER EIGHT

# *What Faith Is*

There are many descriptions of faith, but some of these definitions may be very confusing to many of us. One teacher proclaimed, "I have read the chapter and I will *confound* it." Obviously, he meant to say, "I have read the chapter and I will *expound* it." At least I hope that's what he meant!

We may explain faith to the point that we actually do confound others. It is possible to explain it in such a way that nobody understands it. In this chapter I hope to explain faith in such a way that you will be able to readily understand what it means.

In many ways faith is the simplest of all things. This may be what makes it more difficult to explain.

Faith is made up of three things: knowledge, belief, and trust. Knowledge comes first. We have to hear about Jesus before we can believe in Him. I must be informed of facts before I can believe them. The Bible says, "So then faith cometh by hearing, and hearing by the word of God" (Rom.10:17).

### Spiritual Knowledge

We must first hear the truth in order to know what we should believe. We must know the name of Jesus before we can trust in Him. A measure of knowledge is essential to faith, so it is important to gain knowledge. God wants us to incline our ears toward Him. So search the Scriptures daily and learn what the Holy Spirit teaches concerning Christ and His salvation. Seek to know God.

The Bible says, "... he that cometh to God must believe that he is, and that he is a rewarder of them that diligently seek him" (Heb.11:6). May the Holy Spirit give you the spirit of knowledge and of the fear of the Lord. Know the gospel, and understand what the good news is. Discover how the Word teaches about forgiveness, a change of heart, adoption into the family of God, and a multitude of other blessings.

Know Jesus Christ and realize that He is the Son of God and the Savior of human beings. He is united to us by His human nature, and yet He is one with God; therefore, He is able to serve as a Mediator between God and us. He is able to lay His hand upon both God and us, and He is the connecting link between the sinner and the Judge of all the earth. Always endeavor to know more and more about Jesus.

Learn about His wonderful sacrifice, as it is depicted in this verse: "God was in Christ, reconciling the world unto himself, not imputing their trespasses unto them; and hath committed unto us the word of reconciliation" (2 Cor.5:19).

Jesus was made a curse for us, as this verse declares: "Christ hath redeemed us from the curse of the law, being made a curse for us: for it is written, Cursed is every one that hangeth on a tree" (Gal.3:13).

Drink deeply from the well of the substitutionary work of Christ, for it contains the sweetest possible comfort for the guilty. Understand these precious words: "For he hath made him to be sin for us, who knew no sin; that we might be made the righteousness of God in him" (2 Cor.5:21). Yes, faith begins with knowledge.

### Belief

After we have obtained spiritual knowledge, our minds will begin to believe that the things we've heard, read, and learned are true. Our souls will begin to believe that God *is* and that He hears the cries of our hearts. We will begin to believe that the Gospel of Jesus Christ comes from God and that justification by faith is the grand truth which God has revealed to us through the Holy Spirit in these last days.

Then our hearts will begin to believe that Jesus is truly our God and Savior, our Redeemer, the Prophet, the Priest, and the King of His people. All this will be accepted as sure truth, never to be called into question again.

I pray that you will see this and firmly believe that, "... the blood of Jesus Christ his Son cleanseth us from all sin" (1 John 1:7). I pray that you will understand that His sacrifice is complete and has been fully accepted by God on your behalf. Therefore, because you believe in Jesus Christ, you shall not be condemned. Believe these truths, because they reveal the difference between common faith and saving faith. Believe God's witness just as you believe the testimony of your father or your friend, and remember these words from John: "If we receive the witness of men, the witness of God is greater" (1 John 5:9).

### Trust

Now you have gained spiritual and scriptural knowledge and you have made advances in faith. The next ingredient in this process is trust. Commit yourself to the merciful God. Rest your hope in the gracious gospel. Trust your soul to the Savior. Be cleansed of your sins by His atoning blood. Accept His perfect righteousness. Trust in the lifeblood of faith, and remember there is no saving faith without it.

Puritans used to explain faith by using the word "recumbency," which means "leaning upon something." This is a good picture of what we need to do—to lean all of our weight upon the Lord Jesus Christ. Perhaps a better illustration would be to picture yourself falling prostrate on the Rock of Ages. Cast yourself upon Jesus. Rest in Him, and commit yourself to Him. This is what I mean by exercising saving faith. Faith is not a blind thing, for faith, as we have pointed out, begins with knowledge. Faith is not a speculative thing either, for it believes facts that are sure and certain. Faith is not a dreamy, unpractical thing, for it trusts and stakes its destiny upon the truth of revelation.

Let's continue looking at what faith is. *Faith is believing that Christ is what He is said to be and that He will do what He has promised to do.* True faith enables us to expect these things of Him. The Scriptures declare that Jesus is God in human flesh. He is perfect in His character. He has been made a sin-offering for us. He bore our sins in His own body on the cross.

The Bible tells us that Jesus has finished transgression; He has made an end of sin and brought everlasting righteousness to us. He died on the cross and rose from the dead. Now He "… ever liveth to make intercession" (Heb.7:25) for us. He has entered into glory and has taken possession of Heaven in behalf of His people. In the near future He will come again "… to judge the earth: with righteousness shall he judge the world, and the people with equity" (Ps.98:9).

We must firmly believe these truths. We must believe the testimony of the Father, who said this about Jesus: "Thou art my beloved Son; in thee I am well pleased" (Luke 3:22). The Holy Spirit bore similar witness about Jesus in the Word of God, through miracles, and by His working in the hearts of people. The testimony of the Father and the Holy Spirit are completely true in every respect.

Faith also believes that Jesus Christ will do what He has promised. One thing He promised is that He will never cast out those who come to Him in faith. Faith believes everything Jesus said. For example, it believes this promise: "But whosoever drinketh of the water that I shall give him shall never thirst; but the water that I shall give him shall be in him a well of water springing up into everlasting life" (John 4:14).

We must drink the water of life that Jesus gives to us, for it will well up within us and become a stream of holy and everlasting life. Christ will do whatever He has promised. Believe this, and look to Him for pardon, justification, preservation, and eternal glory.

Jesus is what He is said to be, and Jesus will do what He says He will do. Therefore, we must trust Him. This is what you should be saying to yourself: "He will be to me what He says He is, and He will do to me what He has promised to do. I leave myself in the hands of Him who is appointed to save me. I rest upon His promise that He will do everything He has said." This is saving faith, and when you activate this faith in your life, you will have everlasting life. No matter what dangers, difficulties, darkness, depression, infirmities, and sins may come to your life, if you believe in Jesus Christ, you shall never be condemned.

Don't be afraid. Simply believe. Trust in God, and be at rest. Even though you may not understand everything, step forth in faith. Never mind distinctions and definitions. A hungry man eats even when he does not understand the composition of the food or the anatomy of his mouth and digestive tract. He eats because he knows it will keep him alive. A more sophisticated person who thoroughly understands the science of nutrition will die if he or she does not eat, in spite of all his or her accumulated knowledge.

Many of those who are in hell may have understood the doctrine of faith, but they did not believe. On the other hand, those who have trusted in the Lord Jesus have never been cast out, though they may not understand everything about their faith.

Receive the Lord Jesus Christ into your life, and you will live forever!

# CHAPTER NINE

# Illustrations of Faith

In order to help you understand faith more fully, in this chapter I will share some illustrations with you. I believe it is my divine duty to provide you with as much light on this subject as possible, but the Holy Spirit is the One who will enable you to see the truth. I pray that He will open your eyes to the truth, and that you will pray the same prayer for yourself.

Faith is the eye which looks and sees. The eye is able to bring into the mind things that are far away. We can bring the sun, the moon, and the far-off stars into our minds through our eyes. Similarly, it is by trust that we are able to bring the Lord Jesus near to us. Though He is far away in Heaven, He is able to enter our hearts through faith. Look, therefore, to Jesus, as the following line from a lovely hymn encourages you to do:

*There is life in a look at the Crucified One,*
*There is life at this moment for thee.*

Faith is the hand which grasps. In the same way that our hands may take hold of something that is tangible, faith takes hold of the supernatural by appropriating Christ and all the blessings His redemption has provided for us.

51

Faith is the mouth which says, "Jesus is mine."

Faith is the ear that hears of the pardoning blood of Jesus, leading us to cry, "I accept faith as my means of pardon and forgiveness."

Faith is the voice that claims the legacies of the dying Jesus as its own possession.

Faith is the heir of Christ. He has given himself and all that He has in response to faith.

Dear reader, take all that grace has provided for you. This is your rightful inheritance. God has given you this divine permit: "Let him that is athirst come. And whosoever will, let him take the water of life freely" (Rev.22:17).

If someone were to put a treasure in front of you and invite you to take it, you would be foolish not to reach down and grasp it. Realize then that God has put His treasure in front of you. All you need to do is take it.

Faith is the mouth that feeds upon Christ. Before food can nourish us, it must be received into our bodies. Eating and drinking are simple matters. We take food and drink into our mouths, we swallow them, and through the process of digestion, their nutrients are passed into the various parts of our bodies.

Paul writes, "The word is nigh thee, even in thy mouth, and in thy heart" (Rom. 10:8). Yes, the Word of God is near you. All you need to do is swallow it so it will go into your heart and soul.

I pray that these words will whet your appetite for the things of God. A person who is hungry and sees meat in front of him or her does not need to be taught how to eat. Similarly, a heart that hungers and thirsts after Christ will receive Him openly, without having to be taught how to do so. The Bible says, "But as many as received him, to them gave he power to become the sons of God, even to them that believe on his name" (John 1:12). God never refuses anyone, and all who come to Him remain His children forever.

### The Pursuits of Life

The pursuits of life also illustrate faith in many ways. The farmer buries good seed in the earth and expects it both to live and be multiplied. He has faith in the covenant that seedtime and harvest shall not cease, and his faith is rewarded during the time of harvest.

The merchant places his money in a banker's care and puts his trust in the honesty and soundness of the banker and the bank. He entrusts his capital into the hands of another, and feels more secure and at ease in so doing than if he had solid gold locked up in an iron safe.

The sailor trusts himself to the sea. When he swims, he floats restfully on the surface of the ocean. He could not swim at all if he didn't cast himself wholly upon the water.

The goldsmith puts precious metal into the fire, which seems eager to consume it; but when he receives it back, the furnace has actually purified it.

No matter where you are, you will see faith in operation among people and between people and nature. In the same way that we engage in trust in so many daily situations of life, we must learn to trust in God as He has been revealed to us in Jesus Christ.

Faith exists in people in varying degrees. It varies according to a person's knowledge or growth in grace. Sometimes faith is little more than simply clinging to Christ with a sense of dependence and a willingness to depend on Him. When you are on the seashore, you may see various forms of sea life sticking to a rock. You may walk softly up to the rock and strike a mollusk with a rapid blow from your walking stick, knocking it off the rock. However, when you attempt to do the same with the next mollusk, it will cling so tightly to the rock that you will not be able to knock it off. This is because it has been forewarned with regard to your intentions. It heard the blow that struck its neighbor, and so it clings very tightly to the rock. You will not be able to get it off no matter how many times you strike at it. You might actually be more successful in breaking the rock than in removing the mollusk!

The mollusk doesn't have a great deal of knowledge, but it does know that clinging to the rock will keep it safe. It is not acquainted with the geological formation of the rock; nevertheless it clings to the rock in complete trust. The blessing is that it has found something in which it can place its trust, something to which it can cling in safety. It is the same with us. Our Rock is Jesus, and if we learn to cling to Him, He will keep us safe and secure.

All you need to know is that as you cling to Jesus with all your heart and soul, you will experience His peace and safety. Jesus Christ is a strong and mighty Savior, and He is your immovable and immutable rock. Cling to Him for dear life, and you will be saved.

Faith is seen in action when one person relies upon another based on the superior knowledge the other has. This is a higher level of faith than that of the mollusk, because it knows the reason for its dependence and acts upon it. We see an example of this in a blind person who is led by a person with sight. The blind person trusts his or her guide, because they know the guide can see. In trust, therefore, the blind person will walk where he or she is led.

Those who are born blind may not know what sight is, but they will know that sight exists and that it is possessed by a friend or a guide who will lead them. For this reason the blind are able to place their hand in the hand of the guide in trust, faith, and confidence and they are able to follow the leadership that is provided by the guide. Until we receive Jesus, we are spiritually blind. The Bible says, "For we walk by faith, not by sight" (2 Cor.5:7). Jesus said, "Blessed are they that have not seen, and yet have believed" (John 20:29).

We need to entrust our lives to Jesus even though we cannot see Him, because we know who He is and what He can do. We need to trust Him in the same way that a blind person trusts a guide. Jesus will never betray the confidence we place in Him. As you place your faith and trust in Him, remember that He has been made unto us "... wisdom, and righteousness, and sanctification, and redemption" (1 Cor.1:30).

Every boy or girl who goes to school has to exert faith while learning their lessons. The teacher shows them things about geography and teaches them about the form of the earth and the existence of great cities, countries, and empires. They do not know that what is being taught is true, but they do believe the teacher and the books they read. If you are to be saved, you must do the same. You must simply believe in what Jesus your Master Teacher tells you. You believe because He tells you it is so, and you entrust your life to Him because He has promised to give you salvation.

Almost everything you and I know has come to us by faith. A scientific discovery is made, and we are sure of it, because certain scientific authorities have reported it to us. The reputations they've established help us to trust in them. We may never have seen their experiments, but we believe their witness.

You must do the same with Jesus, because He teaches you certain truths about what it means to be His disciple. Believe His words. He has performed many mighty acts in your behalf, so you know you can trust in Him. He is infinitely superior to you, and He presents Himself as your

Master and Lord. If you will receive Him and His words, you shall be saved!

### Faith That Grows From Love

There is a higher form of faith than the ones we've been discussing. This kind of faith grows out of love. Why does a boy trust his father? It's because he knows his father loves him. Blessed and happy are those who have a sweet faith in Jesus that is intertwined with deep affection for Him, for out of this will develop a restful confidence. All lovers of Jesus are charmed by His character, delighted with His mission, and carried away by His loving-kindness in their lives. Because of these things, they cannot help but trust Him.

Imagine a lady who is the wife of a very eminent physician. She becomes the victim of a very serious illness. Even so, she is wonderfully calm and quiet, because she knows that her husband is a leading authority regarding her malady. She knows that he has brought healing to thousands of people who have had the same illness as herself.

In light of this knowledge she is not perturbed, because she feels perfectly safe in the hands of her husband, a man who is very dear to her. She knows that love and skill are blended perfectly in his life. Her faith is both reasonable and natural, and her husband deserves it.

This is the kind of faith that the happiest believers exercise toward Christ. There is no physician like Him, and no one can save us, except Him. He loves us and we love Him, and this enables us to put ourselves into His hands, to accept whatever He prescribes for us, and to do whatever He wants us to do. We feel certain that nothing can go wrong when we allow Him to be the Director of our affairs. We are aware that He loves us with an everlasting love, and because He does, He will not let us perish or suffer any needless pain.

### Faith—the Root of Obedience

Faith is the root of obedience, as we can easily see while we observe the affairs of daily life. When a captain trusts a pilot to steer his vessel into port, the captain is still managing the vessel because he knows the pilot will proceed according to his direction. When travelers trust a guide to conduct them through a difficult pass in the mountains, they will follow the track that their guide has mapped out. When patients believe in their physician, they will carefully follow the doctor's prescriptions and orders.

Faith that refuses to obey the commands of the Savior is a mere pretense, and it will never save the human soul. We must trust Jesus to save us, and He will give us the directions we need to find the path to salvation. When we follow His directions, we are saved. So trust Jesus, and prove your trust in Him by obeying Him in whatever He directs you to do.

### Assured Knowledge

Another notable form of faith is derived from assured knowledge, which is developed by growth in grace. This faith believes in Christ because it knows Him and trusts Him. This kind of faith has proved Jesus to be infallibly faithful. One elderly Christian was in the habit of writing the letters "T" and "P" in the margins of her Bible whenever she had tried and proved ("T" and "P") God's promises. It is not hard to trust a tried and proved Savior. Though you may not be able to do this fully yet, the time will come when you are able to do so implicitly.

Everything must have a beginning. You will rise to strong faith in due time. Such mature faith does not ask for signs and wonders, but it believes bravely. As an example, let's take a look at the example provided by a master mariner. I have often wondered at such an individual's faith. He loosens his cable and steams away from land. For days, weeks, and even months he never sees sail or shore; yet he continues day and night without fear.

Eventually he ends up at the proper destination. How did he find his way over the trackless deep? He trusted in his compass, his nautical almanac, his telescope, and the heavenly bodies. Without sighting land, he obeyed their guidance and was able to steer the vessel into port. This is a truly wonderful thing.

There is a spiritual lesson in this as well. It is a very blessed thing to leave the shores of sight and feeling and say goodbye to inward feelings, cheering providences, signs, tokens, etc. It is glorious to be far out on the ocean of divine love, believing in God, and steering toward Heaven by the direction of our compass, the Word of God.

Again I implore you to put your trust in God and in Christ Jesus. They will lead you safely home and give you joyous confidence. Come to Him at once.

# CHAPTER TEN

# Faith—the Channel of Salvation

Why has faith been selected to be the channel of salvation? Why weren't love, hope, patience, or joy selected to serve in this way?

As far as I am able to ascertain, faith has been selected to be the channel of grace because there is a natural adaptation in faith that is to be used by the receiver. Suppose that I am about to give a donation to a poor man. Why do I put it into his hands? Well, for one thing, it wouldn't be right to put it in his ear or upon his foot. The hand was designed to receive things.

It is the same with faith, which is the "hand" that is to be used in receiving things from God. We receive God's grace with the hand of faith.

The hand of faith that receives Christ is similar to children receiving an apple in their hands. You hold the apple out to the child and they must step toward you in order to receive it from you. This is a mixture of faith and receiving on the child's part.

It is the same with someone who wants to receive salvation. What the child's hand is to the apple, your faith is to salvation. The child's hand does not make the apple, improve the apple, or deserve the apple; it simply takes it. Similarly, faith has been chosen and designed by God to be the hand with which you receive salvation. Your hand neither creates nor helps in salvation, but is content to humbly receive it.

Someone has said, "Faith is the tongue that begs pardon, the hand which receives it, and the eye which sees it; but it is not the price which buys it." Faith never makes its own plea, but rests all its argument on the blood of Christ. It is a good servant to be used in bringing the riches of the Lord Jesus to the soul, because it acknowledges where they come from and realizes that grace alone entrusted these riches to it.

Faith gives all the glory to God. It is of faith that it might be of grace, and it is of grace that there might be no boasting, for God cannot endure pride. God sees the proud from a distance, and He has no desire to get closer to them. Therefore, He will not give people salvation in any way that will suggest or foster pride. Paul writes, "For by grace are ye saved through faith; and that not of yourselves: it is the gift of God: not of works, lest any man should boast" (Eph. 2:8-9).

Faith excludes all boasting. The hand that receives charity does not say, "I am to be thanked for accepting the gift," for that would be absurd. When the hand puts bread into the mouth, it does not say to the body, "Thank me, for I feed you." It is a very simple thing that the hand does, but it is a very necessary thing as well. The hand does not take glory for itself; it simply realizes that it is the means whereby the body will receive food.

God has selected faith as the means for receiving the unspeakable gift of His grace. Faith cannot take any credit to itself for this, but must adore the gracious God who is the Giver of every good and perfect gift. (See James 1:17.) Faith sets the crown upon the right head, and Jesus sets the crown upon the head of faith. He said, "Thy faith hath saved thee; go in peace" (Luke 7:50).

### Our Connection with God

Another reason why God has selected faith to be the channel of salvation is that it is a sure method, and it links us with God. When a person confides in God, a point of union is established between them, and that union guarantees blessing. Faith saves us because it makes us cling to God and so brings us into connection with Him.

Something that happened at Niagara Falls provides us with a good example of this. Many years ago a boat was upset on the river just above the falls, and two men were rapidly carried down the current toward the precipice. People on the shore threw a rope to them and both men seized it. One of the men held tightly to the rope and was pulled safely to shore, but the other man, upon seeing a log floating nearby, let go of the rope and held on to the log, for it was bigger than the rope and seemed safer.

This was a big mistake for the second man, for the log, having no contact with the shore, soon shot over the falls, and the man was killed on the rocks below! The size of the log had been of no benefit to him; it needed a connection with the shore to assure his safety.

In the same way, when someone trusts in works or sacraments or other things instead of trusting in Christ, they will not be saved, because those things will not give them any connection to God. Faith, however, though it may sometimes seem to be but a thin thread, is in the hands of the great God who is on the shore. His infinite power courses through that lifeline and keeps the person from destruction. Oh, the blessedness of faith, because it unites us with God!

### Faith Touches the Springs of Action

Faith was selected to be the channel of grace because it touches the springs of action. Even in common things, faith is at work. Faith is involved in almost everything we do. As I walk across my study, I exercise faith that my legs will carry me. A person eats because he or she believes that food is necessary. A person goes into business because he or she believes in the value of money. A person accepts a check because he or she believes the bank will honor it.

Columbus discovered America because he believed that another continent existed beyond the ocean. The Pilgrim Fathers went to the New World and built a colony there because they believed God would be with them. Most great deeds have been cultivated by faith. Faith works wonders through the people in whom it dwells.

Faith in its natural form is an all-prevailing force, and it enters into almost all human actions. The person who derides faith in God is someone who exercises an evil form of faith, but he or she is still using faith.

God gives His salvation to us through faith, because by creating faith within us, He touches the real mainspring of our emotions and actions. In a sense, He has taken control of the "battery" within us, and now He can send His sacred current through us to every part of our nature.

When we believe in Christ and have allowed our hearts to become His possession, we are saved from sin, and we have been moved toward repentance, holiness, zeal, prayer, consecration, and every other gracious thing. Someone said, "What oil is to the wheels, what weights are to a clock, what wings are to a bird, what sails are to a ship, faith is to all holy duties and services." So have faith, and all other graces will follow and continue to hold their course.

### Faith Works by Love

Faith has the power of working by love. It influences the affections toward God, and points our hearts toward the best things. He who believes in God will love God without question. Faith is an act of the understanding, but it proceeds from the heart. The Bible says, "For with the heart man believeth unto righteousness; and with the mouth confession is made unto salvation" (Rom.10:10).

God gives salvation to us through faith, because faith resides next to our affections and is very close to love. Love is the parent of every holy feeling and act. Love for God is obedience, and love for God is holiness. To love God and to love man is to be conformed to the very image of Christ, and this is salvation.

### Faith Creates Peace and Joy

The person who has faith experiences rest, tranquility, gladness, and joy. These benefits of faith help to prepare us for Heaven. God gives all His heavenly gifts to faith. Faith works these qualities into our lives, and furnishes us with armor for the battles of life and with education about the life to come. It enables us to live and die without fear, and it prepares us for both action and suffering. As you can see, faith is the most effective means for God to impart His grace to us and thereby secure us for glory.

Faith does for us what nothing else can do. It gives us joy and peace, and it causes us to enter into God's rest. Doesn't this make you wonder why anyone would try to obtain salvation through any other means? An old preacher once said, "A silly servant who is bidden to open a door, sets his shoulder to it and pushes with all his might; but the door stirs not and he cannot enter, no matter what strength he may use. Another comes with a key, easily unlocks the door, and enters readily. Those who would be saved by works are pushing at heaven's gate without result; but faith is the key which opens the gate at once."

Dear reader, will you not use that key? The Lord commands you to believe in His dear Son. Therefore, you may do so, and in doing so you shall live. This is the promise of the gospel: "He that believeth and is baptized shall be saved" (Mark 16:16).

What can be your objection to a way of salvation which commends itself to the mercy and wisdom of our gracious God?

# CHAPTER ELEVEN

# I Can Do Nothing!

After the anxious heart has accepted the doctrine of the Atonement and learned the great truth that salvation is by faith in the Lord Jesus, it is often troubled with a sense of inability with regard to doing that which is good. Many will groan, "I can do nothing!" They are not using this as an excuse; instead, they are feeling it as a daily burden. Like Paul, these are the people who say, "For I know that in me (that is, in my flesh) dwelleth no good thing: for to will is present with me; but how to perform that which is good I find not" (Rom.7:18).

This attitude seems to nullify the gospel message, for what is the good of food if a hungry man can't get to it? Of what avail is the river of the water of life if one cannot drink from it? This brings to my mind the story of a doctor and a poor woman's child. The physician told the mother that her little one would soon get better under the proper treatment, which included drinking the best wines and spending a season at one of the spas in Germany.

The mother was a widow who could hardly get bread to eat on a daily basis, so this was very disturbing news to her. Similarly, many who hear the words, "Believe and live" may find that it is not as simple as it sounds. To the awakened but poorly instructed believer there seems to be a missing link somewhere in this command. They see Jesus' salvation as though it is far away from them, but they don't know how to reach it. Such a soul is without strength, and it doesn't know what to do. It finds itself within sight of the city of refuge, but it cannot enter through its gates.

This needed strength is provided for in the plan of salvation. The Lord's work is perfect. It begins where we are and asks nothing of us in order for it to be completed. When the Good Samaritan saw the traveler lying alongside the road wounded and half-dead, he did not tell him to rise and come to him. He did not instruct the injured man to get on his donkey and ride to the inn. No, he went to the man, knelt down, and ministered to him. Then he lifted him on his beast and took him to the inn. (See Luke 10:30-37.) The Lord Jesus deals with us in the same way.

So far we have seen that God justifies the ungodly through faith in the precious blood of Jesus Christ. Now we'll take a look at the various conditions in which ungodly people find themselves when Jesus works out their salvation. Many people who are spiritually awakened are not only troubled about their sin, but they're also troubled by their moral weakness. They have no strength with which to escape from the mire into which they have fallen. They lament not only over what they have done, but also over what they cannot do. They feel that they are powerless, helpless, and spiritually lifeless. They even feel dead. They feel totally incapable and impotent. They cannot travel the road to Heaven, for they feel that their bones are broken. They need to hear these glorious words: "For when we were yet without strength, in due time Christ died for the ungodly" (Rom. 5:6). Fix your mind on that fact and let it rest there.

Let this one great, gracious, glorious fact settle in your spirit until it permeates all your thoughts and makes you rejoice even though you are without strength: The Lord

Jesus has become your strength and your song, and He has become your salvation. According to the Scriptures, Christ died for the ungodly when they were without strength.

Perhaps you have heard these words hundreds of times, but you have not perceived their true meaning and applied them to your life.

Isn't there something wonderful about them? Jesus did not die for our righteousness, but He did die for our sins. He did not come to save us because we were worth saving, but He came because we were utterly worthless, ruined, and undone. He came because He loved us. He came to redeem the ungodly. Let these truths sink deep within your spirit, for they are able to cheer even the heaviest heart. Let the above-quoted text from the Scriptures lie under your tongue like a sweet morsel until it dissolves and finds its way into your heart and flavors all your thoughts.

### Repentance

Another person might say, "Oh, sir, my want of strength lies mainly in this: that I cannot repent sufficiently." Many people have the wrong idea about repentance. It does not necessarily involve tears and groaning, and it does not mean that you will have to endure deep despair. This is an unreasonable notion that some have regarding repentance.

Unbelief and despair are sins. Therefore, they have nothing to do with true repentance. Even so, many regard them as being essential to the Christian experience. The folk who believe this are in great error. Even so, I do understand where they are coming from, for in the days of my darkness I used to feel the same way. I desired to repent, but I thought I could not do it. Even while thinking these things, though, I was repenting without knowing it.

Odd as it may sound, I felt that I could not feel. I used to get into a corner and weep because I could not weep, and I fell into bitter sorrow because I could not experience sorrow for my sin. What a jumble it all becomes as we try to judge our own condition when we are in a state of unbelief. It is like a blind man trying to look at his own eyes. My heart was melted within me out of fear, because I thought my heart was as hard and adamant as stone. My heart was broken to think that it would not break. Now I can see that I was exhibiting the very thing which I thought I did not possess, but I did not know what was going on within me.

Oh, how I wish I could help others find their way into the light which I now enjoy every day of my life. I would like to say a word or two which would shorten the time of their bewilderment – just a few plain words – and I would pray that the Comforter (the Holy Spirit) would apply those words to their hearts.

The person who truly repents is never satisfied with his or her repentance. We can no more repent perfectly than we can live perfectly. No matter how pure our tears may be, there will always be some dirt in them, and there will always be something to be repented of even in our best repentance. To repent is to change your mind about sin and Christ and all the great things of God. Certainly sorrow is implied in this, but the main point is the turning of your heart from sin to Christ. If you experience this turning, you have discovered the essence of repentance even if no alarm and no despair have cast their shadows in your mind.

If you feel that you cannot repent as you should, it will greatly aid you to firmly believe that Christ died for the ungodly. Think of this truth over and over again. How could anyone continue to be hard-hearted while knowing that Christ died for the ungodly out of His supreme love for them? Let me persuade you to reason with yourself according to the following thought: "Ungodly as I am, though this heart of steel will not relent, though I smite in vain upon my breast, Christ died for such as I am. He died for the ungodly. Oh, that I may truly believe this and feel the power of it upon my flinty heart!"

Blot out every other reflection from your soul, and take time to meditate deeply on this resplendent display of unmerited, unexpected, unequalled love: "Christ died for the ungodly." Read the Scriptures that describe the Lord's death on the cross. You'll find them in the four gospels. Taking a good look at the sufferings Jesus went through in your behalf will melt your heart:

> O Jesus! Sweet the tears I shed,
> While at Thy feet I kneel,
> Gaze on Thy wounded, fainting head,
> And all Thy sorrows feel.
> My heart dissolves to see Thee bleed,
> This heart so hard before;
> I hear Thee for the guilty plead,
> And grief o'erflows the more.
> 'Twas for the sinful Thou didst die,
> And I a sinner stand:
> Convinc'd by Thine expiring eye,
> Slain by Thy pierced hand.
> (Ray Palmer)

Surely the cross is that wonder-making rod which can bring water out of a rock. If you understand the full meaning of the sacrifice of Jesus, you must repent of ever having been opposed to the One who is so full of love. The Bible says, "They shall look upon me whom they have pierced, and they shall mourn for him, as one mourneth for his only son, and shall be in bitterness for him, as one is in bitterness for his firstborn" (Zech.12:10).

Repentance will not make you see Christ, but seeing Christ will give you repentance. The Holy Spirit, by turning us toward Christ, turns us away from sin. Look away, then, from the effect to the cause, from your own repenting to the Lord Jesus, who is exalted on high and will give repentance to you.

One person said to me, "I am tormented with horrible thoughts. Wherever I go, blasphemies steal in upon me. Frequently at my work a dreadful suggestion will force itself upon me; and even when I am on my bed, I am startled from my sleep by whispers from the evil one. I cannot get away from this horrible temptation."

I know what this individual means, for I too have been hunted by this "wolf." A person might as well hope to fight a swarm of flies with a sword as to try to master his or her own thoughts when they are invaded by the devil. A poor, tempted soul who is assailed by satanic suggestions is like a traveler I once read about. This traveler was besieged by a swarm of angry bees that stung his head and ears and many other places on his body. He could not keep them away from him and he could not escape them. They stung him repeatedly and threatened to be the cause of his death.

I am not surprised that you feel you are without the needed strength to stop the horrible and abominable thoughts that Satan brings to your mind, but let me remind you of this verse: "For when we were yet without strength, in due time Christ died for the ungodly" (Rom.5:6). Jesus knew where we were and where we should be. He saw that we could not overcome the prince of the power of the air (Satan) on our own. He knew that we would be greatly disturbed by the enemy, but He died for the ungodly— those who are without strength—because He knew we would need His strength.

Cast the anchor of your faith upon the preceding Bible verse. It is said that Martin Luther was able to decapitate the devil with his own sword. The devil said to him, "You are a sinner."

"Yes," Martin Luther agreed, "but Christ died to save sinners." He then smote the devil with his own sword. Hide yourself in this place of refuge: "Christ died for the ungodly." If you take your stand upon that truth, your blasphemous thoughts, which you cannot drive away in your own strength, will leave by themselves. Satan will see that it is serving no purpose for him to attempt to plague you with such thoughts anymore.

These thoughts are not yours. You hate them. They are from the devil, and he is responsible for them. If you strive against them, they are not your thoughts any more than the curses and falsehoods of rioters in the streets are your thoughts. The devil would like to drive you to despair and distraction with these thoughts, and he would like to keep you from trusting Jesus.

In a way you are similar to the diseased woman who could not reach Jesus because of the throng that surrounded Him. You are surrounded by thoughts that prevent you from reaching out to Jesus. The woman touched the hem of His garment, and she was healed, and you must do the same. (See Matt.9:20.)

Jesus died for all those who are guilty of sin and blasphemy. He will not refuse those who are unwillingly held captive by evil thoughts. Cast yourself upon Him, thoughts and all, and see if He is mighty to save you. He can still those horrible whispers from the fiend and enable you to see them in their true light, so that you will be troubled by them no longer. He can and will save you and give you His perfect peace. Simply trust Him for this and for everything else.

Many people feel that they cannot believe. They cry:

*Oh that I could believe,*
*Then all would easy be;*
*I would, but cannot; Lord, relieve,*

71

*My help must come from thee.*

Many remain in the dark for years because they feel they have no power. They are unable to give up their personal power and find repose in the power of the Lord Jesus. Such people need to realize that they won't get any help from trying to believe. Believing does not come by trying. When God declares that there is salvation in Christ Jesus, we must either believe Him at once or we make a liar of Him. It's not hard to determine which of these choices is the correct one. The witness of God is true, and we are bound by it to believe in Jesus.

Perhaps you have been trying too hard to believe. Be satisfied to have a faith that can hold in its hand this truth: "For when we were yet without strength, in due time Christ died for the ungodly" (Rom.5:6). The Lord Jesus laid down His life for those who did not believe in Him. They weren't able to believe in Him. He died for people who were sinners, not for believers. He came to make these sinners into believers and saints. When He died for them, He viewed them as being without strength.

If you hold to the truth that Christ died for the ungodly and truly believe it, your faith will save you. If you will trust your soul to Jesus, who died for the ungodly, even though you cannot believe all things, move mountains, nor do any other marvelous works, you are still saved. It is not great faith, but true faith that saves you; and salvation does not lie in the faith, but in the Christ in whom faith trusts. Faith as a grain of mustard seed will bring salvation to you. It is not the measure of faith, but the sincerity of faith that must be considered. People will always believe what they know to be true, and you know Jesus to be true, so you can believe in Him.

The cross, which is the object of faith, is also, by the power of the Holy Spirit, the cause of it. Look at the dying

Savior until faith springs up in your heart. Calvary is the best place of all for the building up of confidence and faith. The very atmosphere of that sacred hill brings health to trembling faith. Many a person who has stood at the foot of the cross has said:

*While I view Thee, wounded, grieving,*
*Breathless on the cursed tree,*
*Lord, I feel my heart believing*
*That Thou suffer'dst thus for me.*

### Christ Died for the Ungodly

Someone might cry, "Alas! My want of strength lies in this direction, that I cannot quit my sin, and I know that I cannot go to Heaven and carry my sin with me." I am glad that this person knows this, for it is quite true. You must be divorced from your sin in order to be married to Christ.

Young John Bunyan was on the sports green one Sunday when this thought came to his mind: "Wilt thou have thy sins and go to hell, or wilt thou quit thy sins and go to Heaven?" This brought the young man to a standstill, and it is a question that each one of us will have to answer, because we cannot continue in sin and still go to Heaven.

You must either quit sin or you must quit hope. You might reply to this by saying, "Yes, I am willing enough. To will is present with me, but how to perform that which I would I find not. Sin masters me, and then I have no strength."

At such a time you need to remember this text: "For when we were yet without strength, in due time Christ died for the ungodly" (Rom.5:6). Can you believe this Scripture? God said it, and it is a fact. Therefore, you need to hold on to it firmly, for it is your only hope. Believe it and trust

Jesus, and you will find the power you need to slay your sin. Apart from Him, however, the armed strong man (the devil) will hold you as his bond-slave forever.

I know what I am writing about, for I tried repeatedly to overcome my own sinfulness and failed. My evil propensities were too numerous to overcome. Finally, I cast my guilty soul on Jesus, and I learned a conquering principle that helped me to overcome my sinful self. The doctrine of the cross is very useful for slaying sin. In the same way that warriors of old would use their huge, two-handed swords to mow down their foes at every stroke, we can use faith to overcome the enemy. Faith in our Friend, Jesus, overcomes all evil. If Christ died for me, ungodly as I am and without strength as I am, then I cannot live in sin any longer. Instead, I will rouse myself to love and serve the One who has redeemed me from sin. I can no longer trifle with the evil which caused my best Friend to die. I must be holy for His sake. How can I live in sin when He has died to save me from it?

There is tremendous help in this for those who are without strength. You can know and believe that Christ died for the ungodly, including you. Have you caught this idea yet? For some reason it is a very difficult concept for our darkened, prejudiced, and unbelieving minds to embrace. Sometimes when I've preached, I've thought that I presented the gospel so clearly that everyone would see it and understand it, but then I learned that even intelligent hearers had failed to grasp what I was saying.

Converts will often say that they did not know the gospel until a certain day in their lives even though they had heard it proclaimed for several years! The gospel remains unknown to many, not because it has not been proclaimed, but because it has not been revealed personally to them. The Holy Spirit is ready to give this revelation to those who ask Him. I pray that He will do so as I quote once more from this text: "Christ died for the ungodly."

One man told me, "Oh, sir, my weakness lies in this, that I do not seem to keep a single mind! I hear the word on a Sunday, and I am impressed, but during the week I meet with an evil companion, and my good feelings are all gone. My fellow workmen do not believe in anything, and they say such terrible things, and I do not know how to answer them, and so I find myself knocked over!"

I know this man very well, and I tremble for him. At the same time, however, I realize that if he is really sincere, his weakness can be met by God's grace. The Holy Spirit can cast the evil spirit of fear out of this man. He can make any coward brave. All it takes is for the man to realize that he must not remain in such a deplorable state. It is never good to be mean and beggarly toward oneself.

I would say to this man, "Stand upright and take a good look at yourself. See if you were meant to be like a toad under a plow, so afraid that you don't know whether to move or to stand still. Have a mind of your own.

"Though I might do many things to please my friends, I would never go to hell to please them! It is never good to lose the friendship of God in order to stay on good terms with human beings."

The man might respond by saying, "I know that, but still, though I know it, I cannot pluck up the necessary courage. I cannot show my colors to them. I cannot stand fast!"

I would respond with the verse we've repeated several times in this chapter: "For when we were yet without strength, in due time Christ died for the ungodly" (Rom.5:6).

Peter might have said something like this to the man, "The Lord Jesus died for me even when I was such a poor, weak creature that the maid who kept the fire drove me to lie and to swear that I did not know the Lord."

Yes, Jesus died for those who forsook Him and fled. Your way out of cowardice is found in the above verse. Christ died for *you*. When this gets firmly planted in your soul, you will be able to die for Him if need be. You will be able to say, "I cannot be ashamed of Him who died for me."

Dauntless courage is yours through Christ. Look at the saints who had to face death during the age of martyrs. In those early days of the Church, men, women, and children were not only ready to die for Christ, but they even grew eager to suffer for Him! They presented themselves by the hundreds at the judgment seats of their rulers, and as they did so, they confessed Christ.

A deep sense of the love of Christ for you will lift your mind above all fear of what others can do to you. I pray that this will inspire you with a brave, new resolve to take your stand on the Lord's side and be His follower to the end.

# CHAPTER TWELVE

# Ever-increasing Faith

This chapter deals with ways to increase your faith. Many people say that they want to believe, but cannot. Let's take a practical look at this issue.

Someone might ask, "What should I do in order to believe?" When one person was asked to share the best way to do a certain simple act, he replied that the best way is to do it at once. The shortest way to believe is simply to believe. When the Holy Spirit leads you, you will believe as soon as the truth is set before you. You will believe simply because it is true. The command is clear: "Believe on the Lord Jesus Christ, and thou shalt be saved" (Acts 16:31). It is useless to evade this truth with all kinds of questions and quibbles. The order is plain, and it must be obeyed.

### Listen to the Word of God

However, if you still have difficulty in believing, take it before God in prayer. Tell the great Father what is puzzling you, and beg Him to solve the question by His Holy Spirit. When I cannot believe a statement I find in a book, I may seek an answer from its author. I'm sure his or her answer will satisfy me. It is the same with the Bible. Its Author is God himself, and He will make it clear to you. The Lord is willing to make himself known to you, so go to Him and let Him do so. Go into your prayer closet and cry,

"O Holy Spirit, lead me into the truth! Teach me the things that I do not know."

If faith seems difficult to you, the Holy Spirit will enable you to believe if you hear very frequently and earnestly that which you are commanded to believe. We believe many things because we have heard them so often. If you hear something several times a day, are you not likely to believe it? Some have even believed very unlikely things through this method. The Bible says, "Faith cometh by hearing, and hearing by the word of God" (Rom.10:17).

Therefore, listen to the Word of God and hear it often. If you will earnestly and attentively hear the gospel, you will begin to believe what you hear through the power of the Holy Spirit. Be sure, though, that you are listening to the gospel, and not to other things which are designed to distract and worry you.

### Listen to the Testimonies of Others

Consider also the testimony of other people. The Samaritans believed because of what the woman told them about Jesus. Likewise, many of our beliefs come from the testimonies of others. I believe, for example, that Japan exists, even though I have never traveled there. Others, however, have been there, and they have told me about it. Therefore, I believe it truly does exist.

I believe that I shall die one day even though I've never died. However, a great many people that I've known have died, and this leads me to believe that I shall die as well. The experience and testimonies of others helps me to believe this fact.

Therefore, I want to encourage you to listen to others who will tell you how they were saved, pardoned, and changed in character by the Lord. If you will look into this deeply enough, you will find someone very much like yourself who was saved. If you have been a thief, you can find a thief who has had his or her sins washed away by the blood of Jesus. If you have been sexually immoral, you will find others who have fallen in that same way and were saved. If you are in despair, you will find other people who were hopeless and were saved.

These people will be happy to tell you how the Lord delivered them. As you listen to their testimonies, the Holy Spirit will lead you to believe. A missionary once told the story of an African who could not believe something the missionary had told him. The missionary told him that water could become so hard that you could walk on it, but the African could not believe this. He said that he had believed almost everything else the missionary had told him, but this was too much for him to believe.

The missionary then took the man to England. On one frosty day the river froze, but the African would not walk on the ice. He knew that it was a deep river, and he felt certain that he would drown if he attempted to walk on it. He could not be induced to walk on the river until the missionary and other friends went out on the ice. By seeing others venture out so successfully, he was persuaded to give it a try. He then knew that water could become so hard that you could walk upon it.

In the same way, when you see others who have believed in the Lamb of God and you have observed their peace and joy, you will be gently led to believe as well. The experience of others is one way the Lord helps us to find faith. You have either to believe in Jesus or die; there is no other choice regarding eternal life.

### Respond to God's Authority

Note the authority upon which you are commanded to believe. This will greatly help you to find faith. The authority is not mine; if it were, you could reject it. However, it is the authority of the Lord God that commands you to believe.

He bids you to believe in Jesus Christ, and you must never refuse to obey your Maker.

The story is told of a company foreman who had often heard the gospel of Jesus Christ, but he was afraid that he might not ever be able come to Christ. One day his employer sent a card to him. It said, "Come to my house immediately after work."

When the foreman appeared at the employer's door, the boss came out and said in a rough tone of voice, "What do you want, John? Why are you troubling me at this hour? Work is over, so what right have you to be here?"

"Sir," the foreman replied, "I had a card from you that invited me to come here after work."

His boss responded, "Do you mean to say that merely because you had a card from me, you are to come up to my house and call me out after business hours?"

"Well, sir," replied the foreman, "I do not understand you, but it seems to me that, because you sent for me, I had a right to come."

"Come in, John," the employer offered. "I have another message I want to read to you."

His boss sat down and read these words, "Come unto me, all ye that labour and are heavy laden, and I will give your rest" (Matt.11:28). He paused, then went on, "Do you think after such a message from Christ that you can be wrong in coming to Him?"

John's eyes were opened to the truth of the gospel, and he believed in the Lord Jesus unto eternal life, because he now had good warrant and authority for believing in Him. You have that same authority, dear reader. So come to Christ, for the Lord wants you to trust Him.

This story by itself ought to be enough to lead you to believe, but if it is not, then think over what it is that you have to believe – that the Lord Jesus Christ suffered in your place, and He is able to save all who trust Him. This is the most blessed fact that men were ever told to believe, and it is the most suitable, comforting, and divine truth that was ever set before us. Think much upon this truth, and search for the grace and love that it represents. Study the four gospels – Matthew, Mark, Luke, and John – and study the epistles of Paul, Peter, and John. You will find their message to be a most credible one indeed.

### Think Upon the Person of Christ

Also, think upon the Person of Jesus Christ. Think of who He is, what He did, where He is, and what He is. How could you ever doubt Him? Jesus has done nothing to deserve distrust, so it is almost cruel for you to distrust Him. It should be easy for you to rely on Him. Why crucify Him again with unbelief? The ones who crucified Him made Him a martyr, but you make Him a liar through unbelief.

Do not ask, "How can I believe?" Instead, answer this question: "How can I not believe?"

Submit yourself to God. Prejudice and pride are at the bottom of your disbelief. May the Spirit of God take away your enmity and make you yield to Him. You are a proud rebel, and that is why you do not believe your God. Give up your rebellion. Throw down your weapons. Yield to the Lord, and surrender to your King.

When you cry, "Lord, I yield," and really do so within your heart, faith will follow. The reason it has not done so up till now is because you still have a quarrel with God, and you want your own way, not His. For these reasons you cannot believe. May the Holy Spirit work secretly but effectually within you and bring you at this very moment to believe in the Lord Jesus Christ. Amen.

# CHAPTER THIRTEEN

# The Role of the Holy Spirit

Jesus said, "Ye must be born again" (John 3:7). Many people despair when they read these words, for they fear that such a commandment is beyond their ability. They're right about this, for the new birth does not come from them; it comes from above. It is the work of the Holy Spirit in their lives.

The new birth is a supernatural experience; a human being cannot make it happen. In John 3 Jesus teaches about salvation by faith. He says, "Verily, verily, I say unto thee, except a man be born again, he cannot see the kingdom of God" (John 3:3).

Jesus continues to develop this theme later in that same chapter: "And as Moses lifted up the serpent in the wilderness, even so must the Son of man be lifted up: that whosoever believeth in him should not perish, but have eternal life" (John 3:14-15).

A few verses later, He says, "He that believeth on him is not condemned: but he that believeth not is condemned already, because he hath not believed in the name of the only begotten Son of God" (John 3:18).

From these verses it is safe to conclude that the Lord will give to those who believe all that is declared to be necessary for salvation. The Lord does, in fact, produce the new birth in all who believe in Jesus. From then on, their believing is the surest evidence that they have been born again.

We trust in Jesus for what we cannot do for ourselves. If these things were within our own power, why would we need Him? Our job is to believe; His job is to create us anew. He will not believe for us, and we cannot do the work of regeneration that is necessary. It is enough for us to obey His gracious command, and the Lord will work the new birth into us. He went so far as to die on the cross of Calvary for us, so we can be sure that He will give us all things that are needed for our eternal safety.

### Newness of Life

The Holy Spirit works in our lives to change our hearts and give us newness of life. His work is secret and mysterious, but it is very efficacious as well. We know what He has done in a person's life by looking at the results —the fruit that the renewed person brings forth.

In the same way that there are mysteries surrounding a natural birth, there are also mysteries surrounding the new birth. These "mysteries" center on the sacred operations of the Holy Spirit in a person's life. Jesus said, "The wind bloweth where it listeth, and thou hearest the sound thereof, but canst not tell whence it cometh, and whither it goeth: so is every one that is born of the Spirit" (John 3:8).

Just because the work of the Holy Spirit is mysterious is not a reason to refuse to believe in Jesus. If a farmer asked a man to sow a field, the man could not excuse his failure to do so by saying that it would be useless to sow unless God caused the seed to grow. He would not be justified in neglecting the tilling of the soil because the secret energy of God alone can create a harvest. No one is hindered in the ordinary pursuits of life by the fact that unless the Lord builds the house, they labor in vain who build it. (See Ps. 127:1.) It is certain that no person who believes in Jesus will ever find that the Holy Spirit will refuse to work in him or her. In fact, the person's believing is the proof that the Spirit is already at work in his or her heart.

### God Works through Providence

God works through providence, but this does not mean that we should sit still. We could not move without the divine power that gives us life and strength. This power is bestowed upon us day by day and minute by minute. It is God's grace at work in our lives.

We repent and we believe, but it is important for us to understand that we could do neither without the enabling power of the Holy Spirit. We forsake sin and we trust in Jesus, and then we realize it is the Lord who is at work within us to will and to do of His own good pleasure.

Some truths which are difficult to explain in words are simpler to understand by way of experience. There is no discrepancy to be found in saying that a person chooses to believe truth and that his or her faith is wrought by the Holy Spirit. The two go hand in hand with each other.

It's a folly for people to puzzle over plain matters while their souls are in danger. No person would refuse to enter a lifeboat because he or she is not certain about the specific gravity of human bodies. Similarly, a starving person would not decline to eat because he or she does not understand the process of nutrition.

Dear reader, if you will not believe until you understand all mysteries, you will never be saved. If you allow your self-invented difficulties to keep you from accepting pardon through your Lord and Savior, you will perish in an eternal condemnation that will be richly deserved. Do not commit spiritual suicide through a passion for discussing philosophical subtleties.

# CHAPTER FOURTEEN

# *My Redeemer Lives!*

Throughout this book I have pointed you to the crucified Christ, who is the hope of the guilty. We need to realize, though, that He rose from the dead and lives eternally. You are not asked to trust a dead Jesus, but One who, though He died for our sins, has risen again for our justification.

You may go to Jesus right now as if you were going to a living friend of yours. He is not a mere memory; He is a continually existent Person who will hear your prayers and answer them. His purpose is to carry on the work for which He laid down His life. He is interceding for sinners at the right hand of the Father, and for this reason He is able to save to the uttermost those who come to God through Him. So come and try the living Savior if you have never done so before.

### *Jesus Is Alive!*

The living Jesus has been raised to great glory and power. He does not sorrow as a humble man before his foes, and He does not labor as the carpenter's son anymore. Our Lord Jesus is exalted far above all principality and power and every name that is named. (See Eph.1:21.) The Father has given all power in Heaven and in earth to

Him. (See Matt. 28:18.) Jesus uses His divine power and authority to carry out His work of grace in our midst.

Peter said, "The God of our fathers raised up Jesus, whom ye slew and hanged on a tree. Him hath God exalted with his right hand to be a Prince and a Saviour, for to give repentance to Israel, and forgiveness of sins" (Acts 5:30-31). The glory that surrounds our risen Lord should breathe hope into every believer's breast.

Jesus is our great Savior. He is the crowned and enthroned Redeemer of mankind. The sovereign prerogative of life and death is vested within Him. The Father has put all men under the government of His Son, the Mediator, so that He can quicken whomever He will. He opens the door, and no man can shut it. At His word the soul which is bound by cords of sin and condemnation can be unloosed in a moment. He stretches out His silver scepter, and whoever touches it lives.

Jesus is alive! He is greater than all foes. Yes, sin, the flesh, and the devil live, but Jesus, our living Savior and Lord, is far more powerful than any enemy, and He has great power to save us.

His exaltation to glory is for us. He is exalted to be a Prince and a Savior, that He may give all that is needed to accomplish the salvation of all who choose to come under His rule. Jesus *has* all that we need, and Jesus *is* all that we need. His abounding grace is truly sufficient for us.

Jesus endured great humiliation on earth, and now He is an exalted Prince in Heaven. As a result of the humiliation He had to go through, He accomplished all the Father's will, and the Father has rewarded Him by raising Him to glory.

Dear reader, raise your eyes to the hills of glory, for your help will come from Jesus who now resides there. Contemplate the high glories of the Prince and Savior. Doesn't it give you a great sense of hope to realize that a

Man is now seated on the throne of the universe? Is it not glorious that the Lord of all is the Savior of sinners? We have a Friend in the courtroom, a Friend who sits on the throne of Heaven. He will use all His influence in behalf of those who entrust their lives into His hands. Read the following verse and gain insight into the living Christ who loves you with an everlasting love:

*He ever lives to intercede*
*Before His Father's face;*
*Give Him, my soul, thy cause to plead,*
*No doubt the Father's grace.*

Come to Him now, dear reader, and commit your cause and your case into His once-pierced hands, which are now glorified with the signet ring of royal power and honor. This great Advocate will never fail you. He will plead for you.

# CHAPTER FIFTEEN

# Repentance and Forgiveness

R epentance and forgiveness are inextricably bound together. In Acts 5:31 we read that Jesus has been exalted "... to give repentance to Israel, and forgiveness of sins." These two blessings come from the sacred hand that was once nailed to the cross, but has now been raised to glory. Repentance and forgiveness are riveted together by the eternal purpose of God. What God has joined together no man should put asunder.

Repentance must go with remission. Think about this for a moment: Pardon of sin should not be given to an impenitent sinner. If an impenitent sinner were pardoned, he or she would feel that it is all right to continue in sin, and such a person would not think about evil very much at all.

If the Lord were to say, "You love sin and live in it, and you are going from bad to worse, but I forgive you," then He would be giving the person a license to keep on sinning. In such a case the very foundations of our social order would be removed and moral anarchy would soon follow.

It's impossible to tell what crimes and mischief would occur if repentance and forgiveness were divided and the sinner remained as fond of his or her sin as before. If we believe in the holiness of God, we will understand that to continue in our sins without repentance would prevent us from being forgiven and cause us to reap the consequences of our stubbornness and obstinacy.

According to the infinite goodness of God, we are promised that if we will forsake our sins, confess our sins, and accept the grace that Jesus Christ has provided for us, God will be faithful and just to forgive us our sins and to cleanse us from all unrighteousness. (See 1 John 1:9.)

However, there can be no promise of mercy for those who continue in their evil ways and refuse to acknowledge their wrongdoings. Surely no rebel can expect the king to pardon his or her treason while he or she remains in open revolt. No one can be so foolish as to imagine that the Judge of all the Earth will put our sins away if we refuse to put them away ourselves.

### The Completeness of Divine Mercy

Repentance must go with forgiveness for the completeness of divine mercy. That mercy which could forgive the sin and let the sinner continue to live in it would be scant and superficial mercy. It would be unequal and deformed mercy. It would be lame and withered mercy.

Which is the greater privilege: cleansing from the guilt of sin, or deliverance from the power of sin? Both are immeasurably great, and neither would have come to us apart from the precious blood of Jesus. To be delivered from the dominion of sin, to be made holy, to be made like God, however, must be the greater of the two, if a comparison must be drawn.

To be forgiven is an immeasurable favor. The Psalmist writes, "Bless the LORD, O my soul: and all that is within me, bless his holy name. Bless the LORD, O my soul, and forget not all his benefits: who forgiveth all thine iniquities; who healeth all thy diseases" (Ps.103:1-3). God forgives all your iniquities when you confess them, forsake them, and repent of them.

If we were forgiven and were permitted to continue to love sin, to riot in iniquity, and to wallow in lust, we wouldn't really need forgiveness after all. In such a case, forgiveness would turn out to be a "poisoned sweet," which would eventually destroy us. To be washed and then to return to wallow in the mire would be pointless. To be pronounced clean and yet have leprosy would be a mockery of mercy. Why would you bring a person out of a sepulcher if he or she were to remain dead? Why would you lead someone to the light if he or she were to remain blind?

Thank God, He forgives our iniquities and heals our diseases. He who washes us from the stains of the *past* also lifts us up from the foul ways of the *present* and keeps us from failing in the *future*. We must joyfully accept both repentance and remission, for they cannot be separated. To divide God's work of grace would be like cutting a living child in half.

Would you be satisfied with one of these mercies alone? Would you be content, dear reader, if God would forgive your sin and then allow you to continue to be as worldly and wicked as before? I think your answer must be "no," because the quickened spirit is more afraid of sin itself than of its punishments and consequences.

This should be the cry of your heart, "Who shall deliver me from the body of this death? Who shall enable me to live above temptation and to become holy, even as God is holy?" Since the unity of repentance and remission agrees with your gracious desires and since it is necessary for the completeness of salvation, make sure that you let it continue to be the cry of your heart.

### The Experience of All Believers

Repentance and forgiveness are joined together in the experience of all believers. There has never been a person who has sincerely repented of his or her sin with believing repentance who has not been forgiven. Similarly, there never has been a person who has been forgiven without repenting of his or her sin.

There never has been and never will be any case of sin being washed away without a person's heart being led to repentance and faith in Jesus Christ. Hatred of sin and a sense of pardon join together in our souls, and they abide together throughout our lives.

Repentance and forgiveness act and react upon each other. The person who is forgiven repents, and the person who repents is assuredly forgiven. Remember that forgiveness leads to repentance, as Hart's hymn proclaims:

*Law and terrors do but harden,*
*All the while they work alone;*
*But a sense of blood-bought pardon*
*Soon dissolves a heart of stone.*

When we are sure that we are forgiven, we will abhor all forms of iniquity. When faith grows into full assurance and we are certain beyond a doubt that the blood of Jesus has washed us whiter than snow, it is then that repentance reaches its greatest height. Repentance grows as faith grows.

Repentance does not involve just days and weeks. It is not a temporary penance, which you want to be finished with as soon as possible. Like faith itself, repentance is the grace of a lifetime.

God's little children repent; and so do fathers, mothers, teenagers, and elderly people. Repentance is the inseparable companion of faith. Tears of repentance glisten in the eye of faith as we walk by faith and not by sight. It is not true repentance if it does not come by way of faith in Jesus Christ. Similarly, it cannot be true faith if it is not tinged with repentance.

Faith and repentance, like conjoined twins, are joined vitally together. We repent in the same proportion that we believe in the forgiving love of Christ. We rejoice in the fullness of the absolution which Jesus has been exalted to bestow upon us in the same proportion as we repent of sin and hate evil. You will never value pardon unless you feel repentance, and you will never taste the deepest draughts of repentance until you know that you are pardoned. The bitterness of repentance and the sweetness of pardon blend together to flavor every gracious life, and they merge together to bring total happiness.

The two covenant gifts of repentance and forgiveness are mutually assured. If I know that I have repented, I know I am forgiven. There is no other way to know that I've been forgiven except that I have turned from my former sinful course (the result of repentance). To be a believer is to be a penitent. Faith and repentance are two spokes in the same wheel and two handles for the same plow.

Repentance has been described as a heart that is broken *for* sin and *from* sin. We could describe it as *turning* and *returning* as well. Certainly, it is a radical change of one's mind that involves sorrow for the past and a resolution to change the future. The following verse helps us to see it more clearly:

> *Repentance is to leave*
> *The sins we loved before;*
> *And show that we in earnest grieve*
> *By doing so no more.*

When this is the case in your life, you will be certain that you are forgiven, for the Lord never made a heart to be broken *for* sin and broken *from* sin without fully pardoning it. If we are enjoying His pardon through the blood of Jesus and are justified by faith and have peace with God through Jesus Christ our Lord, we know that our repentance and faith are proper.

### The Two Pillars:  Repentance and Remission

Do not regard your repentance as the cause of your remission, however, but as the companion of your remission. Do not expect to be able to repent until you see the grace of the Lord Jesus Christ and His readiness to blot out your sin. Keep these blessed things in their proper places and view them in their relation to each other. They are the Jachin and Boaz of a saving experience. By this analogy I mean that they are comparable to Solomon's two pillars, which stood in front of the house of the Lord and formed a majestic entrance for that holy place. (See 2 Chron.3:17.)

No person comes to God unless he or she passes between the two pillars of repentance and remission. The rainbow of covenant grace is bestowed upon your heart in all its beauty when the light of forgiveness has shined upon the tear drops of repentance. Repentance of sin and faith in divine pardon form the warp and woof of the fabric of real conversion.

So, as you've seen in this chapter, forgiveness and repentance flow from the same source; they are given by the same Savior. The Lord Jesus in all His glory bestows both upon the same person. You are unable to find remission and repentance anywhere else. Jesus has both of these blessings ready for you, and He is ready to bestow them freely upon you now. All you have to do is accept them from His hands.

Let it never be forgotten that Jesus has provided all that is necessary for your salvation. Remember this if you are seeking His mercy for your life. Faith is as much the gift of God as is the Savior upon Whom that faith relies. Repentance from sin is as truly the work of grace as is the Atonement, which blots out the stains of sin. Salvation is of grace alone.

We must repent of our sins. If we don't do so, we cannot expect to be saved from the power of sin. The Holy Spirit and the Lord Jesus do not need to repent, but we do. We must let our wills, affections, and emotions work together in the act of repentance. There is a wonderful holy influence that leads us to repentance, melts our hearts, gives contrition, and produces a complete change within us. We must let that influence—the Holy Spirit—have complete sway in our lives.

The Holy Spirit enlightens us so that we can truly see what sin actually is, and that when we see it in the light He provides, we will loathe it. The Spirit of God also turns us toward holiness and makes us appreciate, love, and desire holiness in our lives. He provides us with the impetus we need to head in the direction of holiness and sanctification.

The Holy Spirit works in us to will and to do according to God's good pleasure. (See Phil.2:13.) Therefore, let's submit our spirits to the Holy Spirit, that He may lead us to Jesus, who will freely give us the double benediction of repentance and remission, according to the riches of His grace.

# CHAPTER SIXTEEN

# Repentance Is Possible, Available, and Acceptable

O ur Lord Jesus Christ has gone up to Heaven so that grace could come down to us. His glory makes His grace all the more valuable to us. The Lord did not take a step upward without taking us upward with Him. He has been exalted in order to give us repentance from sin.

The work which our Lord Jesus has done has made repentance possible, available, and acceptable. The Law makes no mention of repentance, but plainly states, "The soul that sinneth, it shall die" (Ezek.18:20). If the Lord Jesus had not died and risen again and ascended unto the Father, our repenting would be worth little. We might feel remorse with all of its horrors, but we would never be able to experience repentance with the hope it brings to the human heart.

Repentance, as a natural impulse, is a common duty that deserves no praise. Indeed, it is usually mingled with a selfish fear of punishment. Had Jesus not done what He did for us, our tears of repentance would have simply been water poured upon the ground. Jesus is now exalted on high, and through His intercession for us, repentance now has meaning and a place before God. In this sense, therefore, it is accurate to say that Jesus gives us repentance, because He puts repentance into a position of acceptance, which it could not have occupied otherwise.

When Jesus was exalted on high, the Spirit of God was poured out to work all needful graces within us. The Holy Spirit creates repentance in us by supernaturally renewing our nature and taking away the heart of stone from our flesh. Repentance does not come from an unwilling nature, but from free and sovereign grace. So don't go to your chamber to smite your breast in order to fetch from a heart of stone feelings that aren't there. Instead, go to Calvary and see how Jesus died. Look upward to the hills from which your help comes. The Holy Spirit has come on purpose so that He might overshadow our spirits and stir repentance within them, even as He once brooded over the chaos and brought forth order. Breathe your prayer to Him in words like these: "Blessed Spirit, dwell with me. Make me tender and lowly of heart, that I may hate sin and unfeignedly repent of it." He will hear your cry and answer you.

Remember, too, that when our Lord Jesus was exalted, He not only gave us repentance by sending the Holy Spirit, but by consecrating all the works of nature and of providence to the great ends of our salvation, so that any one of them may call us to repentance. From the right hand of God, our Lord Jesus rules all things here below and makes them work together for the salvation of His redeemed. He uses both trials and joys, bitterness and sweetness, so that He may produce in sinners a better mind toward their God.

Be thankful for the providence which has made you poor, sick, or sad, for by all this Jesus works in the life of your spirit and turns you back to Himself. The Lord's mercy often rides to the door of our hearts on the black horse of affliction. Jesus uses the whole range of our experience to wean us from earth and woo us to Heaven. Christ is exalted to the throne of Heaven and earth in order that, by all the processes of His providence, He may subdue hard hearts unto the gracious softening of repentance.

In addition, He is at work even now by all His whispers in our consciences, by His inspired Book, by those of us who preach and teach from His Book, and by praying and earnest friends. He can send a word to you, which will strike your rocky heart as if it had been stricken by Moses' rod, and He can cause streams of repentance to flow forth from you. He can bring to your mind some heartbreaking text from the Scriptures, which shall conquer you speedily. He can mysteriously soften you and cause a holy frame of mind to steal over you when you are not looking for it. Be sure of this, that He who has ascended into glory and has been raised into all the splendor and majesty of God, has abundant ways of working repentance in those to whom He grants forgiveness.

He is even now waiting to give repentance to you. Ask Him for it at once.

Observe with much comfort that the Lord Jesus Christ gives this repentance to the most unlikely people in the world. He was exalted to give repentance to Israel. To Israel! In the days when the apostles were speaking and ministering, Israel was the nation that had most grossly sinned against God's light and love. Even so, Jesus has been exalted to give repentance to them! What a marvel of grace!

If you have been brought up in the brightest Christian light and have rejected it, there is still hope for you. If you have sinned against your conscience, against the Holy Spirit, and against the love of Jesus, repentance is still available to you. Though you may be as hard and unbelieving as the people of Israel were, softening may yet come to you, because Jesus has been exalted to give repentance and forgiveness of sins to those who come to Him. It makes me so happy to be able to proclaim such a full gospel to you! I trust it makes you happy to read it.

The hearts of the children of Israel had grown as hard as an adamant stone. The Lord said that Israel would have none of Him, and John writes, "He came unto his own, and his own received him not" (John 1:11).

In spite of all this, Jesus has been exalted for the giving of repentance and remission to the people of Israel and to others as well. You may be a Gentile with a very stubborn heart, and you may have stood against the Lord Jesus for many years. Even so, our Lord can work repentance into your life. Perhaps you will become like William Hone, a once stout-hearted infidel, who yielded to divine love and wrote *The Everyday Book*. When he was subdued by sovereign grace, he wrote these words:

*The proudest heart that ever beat*
*Hath been subdued in me;*
*The wildest will that ever rose*
*To scorn Thy cause and aid Thy foes*
*Is quell'd, my Lord, by Thee.*
*Thy will, and not my will be done,*
*My heart be ever Thine;*
*Confessing Thee the mighty Word,*
*My Saviour Christ, my God, my Lord,*
*Thy cross shall be my sign.*

The Lord can give repentance to the most unlikely people, and He can turn lions into lambs and ravens into doves. Let us look to Him, that this great change may be wrought in us. Assuredly, the contemplation of the death of Christ is one of the surest and speediest methods of gaining repentance. Do not sit down and try to pump up repentance from the dry well of your corrupt nature. It is contrary to the laws of mind to suppose that you can force your soul into that gracious state. Take your heart in prayer to Him who understands it, and say, "Lord, cleanse my heart. Lord, renew my heart. Lord, work repentance within my heart."

The more you try to produce penitent emotions within yourself, the more you will be disappointed, but if you believingly think of Jesus dying for you, repentance will burst forth. So meditate on the Lord's shedding His heart's blood out of His love for you. Set before your mind's eye His agony and His bloody sweat. Look to the cross and the passion of Jesus Christ. As you do so, He who bore all this grief and pain in your behalf will look at you, and He will do for you what He did for Peter, so that you will be able to go out and weep bitterly as the apostle did. He who died for you can, by His gracious Spirit, make you die to sin; and He who has gone into glory on your behalf, can draw your soul after Him, away from evil and toward holiness.

I shall be content to leave this thought with you as the conclusion of this chapter: Do not look beneath the ice to find fire, and don't hope to find repentance in your natural heart. Look instead to the living One; He will give you life and everything you need. Never seek elsewhere for the things that only Jesus can bestow upon you. Remember, Christ is all!

# CHAPTER SEVENTEEN

# The Fear of Not Persevering to the End

A dark fear haunts the minds of many who are coming to Christ. They are afraid that they shall not be able to persevere to the end. I have heard seekers say, "If I were to cast my soul upon Jesus, what would happen if I were to fall back into perdition? I have had good feelings before now, but they have all died away. My goodness has been as the morning cloud and as the early dew. It came on suddenly, lasted for a season, promised much, and vanished away!"

I believe this fear is often the father of the fact, and that some who have been afraid to trust Jesus for all time and eternity have failed because their faith was only temporary, and it never went far enough to save them. They set out trusting in Jesus to a certain extent, but they then began to look to themselves for continuance and perseverance in the heavenward way. Therefore, they set out on their journey in a faulty way and, as a natural consequence of this, they eventually turned back.

If we trust ourselves to hold on to our faith, we will surely fail. No chain is stronger than its weakest link. If Jesus is our hope for everything except one thing, we shall utterly fail, because it is in that one point that we shall not prevail. I have no doubt whatever that a mistake about the perseverance of the saints has prevented many who started out well to falter and fail. What hindered them and kept them from keeping on with their walk of faith? They trusted to themselves, and so they stopped short.

Beware of mixing even a little of self with the mortar you use to build, or you will make it into untempered mortar, and the stones of the building will not hold together. If you look to Christ at the beginning of your Christian life, but then begin to look to yourself for its continuance to the end, you will fail. Jesus is Alpha (the beginning), and be sure that you make Him Omega (the ending) as well. If you begin in the Spirit, you must not hope to be made perfect by the flesh. Begin in the same way that you intend to continue, and go on in the same way that you begin. Let the Lord be everything to you along the way. I pray that the Holy Spirit will give you a very clear idea of where the strength that will preserve you to the day of our Lord's appearing will come from.

### God's Provision

Paul wrote, "So that you come behind in no gift; waiting for the coming of our Lord Jesus Christ: who shall also confirm you unto the end, that ye may be blameless in the day of our Lord Jesus Christ. God is faithful, by whom ye were called unto the fellowship of his Son Jesus Christ our Lord" (1 Cor.1:7-9).

The language Paul uses in this passage tells us about our great need and how God provides for that need. When the Lord makes a provision for His children, He does so because He knows it is needed. No superfluities encumber the covenant of grace. Golden shields that were never used hung in Solomon's courts, but everything in God's armory is used and useful. We surely need everything that God has provided for us.

Between this present hour and the consummation of all things, every promise of God and every provision that is found in His covenant of grace will be needed and used. The urgent needs of the believing soul are confirmation, continuance, final perseverance, and preservation to the end. God has made provision for all of these.

These are the great necessities for every believer, including the most advanced, as Paul points out in his letter to the Corinthians: "I thank my God always on your behalf, for the grace of God which is given you by Jesus Christ" (1 Cor.1:4). Here, the great apostle is writing to the mature saints in Corinth. These people knew they had a daily need for new grace in their lives to enable them to hold on and hold out. They knew they needed God's grace to make them into conquerors.

If you were not a saint, you would not need grace; but you are a child of God, and therefore you feel the demands of the spiritual life on a daily basis. A marble statue requires no food, but every living person both hungers and thirsts, and he or she rejoices when food and drink become available, for they would faint by the wayside without these necessities. The believer's personal wants and needs make it inevitable that he or she should daily draw from the great source of all supplies—God's abounding grace. Whatever would we do if we could not go to God for what we need?

This need of daily grace is for all believers, including the most gifted saints. The people at Corinth were enriched with all utterance and all knowledge. They needed to be confirmed to the end or else their gifts and attainments would prove to be their ruin. Even if we had the tongues of men and of angels but had no grace, where would we be? If we had all experience and became church leaders and were taught by God to understand all mysteries, where would we be without grace? We could not live a single day without divine life flowing into us from our covenant Head. How could we hope to hold on for a single hour, to say nothing of a lifetime, unless the Lord should keep us? He who began the good work in us must perform it unto the day of Christ, or our lives will prove to be painful failures. (See Phil.1:6.)

Our great necessity for the grace of God in our lives arises very much from our own selves. In some there is a painful fear that they shall not persevere in grace because they know their own fickleness. Certain persons seem to be constitutionally unstable. Some are by nature conservative, if not completely obstinate. Others are naturally changeable and volatile. Like butterflies, they flit from flower to flower until they visit all the beauties of the garden without settling down upon any of them. They are never in one place long enough to do any good, not even in their businesses or their intellectual pursuits. Such persons may well be afraid that ten, twenty, thirty, forty, or perhaps fifty years of continuous religious watchfulness will prove to be too much for them. We regularly see people who join one church and then another, and on and on they go. They do everything by turns, and stay in one place only for a short while. These folk have a double need to pray that they may be divinely confirmed, and that God will make them steadfast and unmovable so that they will always abound in the work of the Lord. (See 1 Cor.15:58).

All of us, even if we do not have a constitutional temptation toward fickleness, must feel our own weaknesses if we are truly quickened by God. Dear reader, do you not find enough in a single day to make you stumble? You that desire to walk in perfect holiness, as I trust you do, and you who have set a high standard of Christian living before you, do you not find that before the breakfast things are cleared away from the table, you have displayed enough folly to make you ashamed of yourself?

If we were to shut ourselves within a solitary cell and live like a hermit, we would still encounter temptation. This is true because we cannot escape from ourselves and the various things that entice us. We know our own hearts, and this knowledge helps us to understand that we must remain humble and watchful before God. If He does not confirm us, it is because we are so weak that we constantly stumble and fall. In such a case, we have not been overturned by an enemy, but we have been overturned by our own carelessness. Lord, be our strength, for we are weakness itself.

### Overcoming Weariness

In addition to the previous areas of concern that I've cited, I know that many experience the weariness that comes from living a long life. When we begin our Christian walk, we mount up with wings as eagles, we run without weariness, and we walk without fainting. (We do these things on our best days at least.)

Eventually, however, our pace begins to slow down, but we think it's because our Christian life can be better sustained in this way. I pray that God will continue to give you the energy of youth through the power of the Holy Spirit, not as the result of proud flesh. The person who has been on the road to Heaven for a long time finds that there is a good reason why he or she was promised shoes of iron and brass, for the road is very rough indeed.

This person has also discovered that he or she must climb "hills of difficulty" and go through "valleys of humiliation." Along the way, he or she discovered a "vale of deathshade," and, worse yet, a "vanity fair." Each of these obstacles and challenges had to be surmounted before he or she could continue. Likewise, this person has entered "castles of despair," where many believers have been. Considering all these things, the person of God who holds out to the end in the way of holiness truly is someone who should be wondered at.

The days of a Christian's life are like threads of mercy upon the golden string of divine faithfulness. In Heaven we shall share the unsearchable riches of Christ, which He lavished upon us and we enjoyed here below with angels, principalities, and powers. We have been kept alive even when we were on the brink of death. Our spiritual lives have been a flame burning in the midst of the sea, and a stone that has remained suspended in the air. The universe will be amazed when we walk through the pearly gates as blameless men and women in the day of our Lord Jesus Christ. We ought to continue to be full of grateful wonder over being kept just one hour, and I trust we are.

Portions of what I'm sharing in this chapter may be anxiety-producing to some, but I have more to say. We have to think of the world in which we live. It is a howling wilderness to many of God's people. Some of us are great beneficiaries of the providence of God, but others seem less fortunate. We begin our days with prayer, and we hear the voice of holy song being raised often in our homes. However, many good people have barely risen from their knees before they are confronted with blasphemy. They go to work, and all day long they are vexed by the filthy conversations they hear. These people are like Lot was in Sodom.

Can you even walk along the street without hearing foul language? The world is no friend to grace. The best we can do with this world is to get through it as quickly as we possibly can, for we dwell in enemy country. There is a robber lurking behind every bush. Everywhere we go we need to keep our sword drawn and firmly fixed in our hands. We need to use the weapon of prayer constantly. As we walk through this world, we need to contend for every inch of ground we traverse. O God, help us and confirm us to the end.

True religion is supernatural at its beginning, supernatural in its continuance, and supernatural at its close. It is the work of God from beginning to end. There is a great need for the hand of the Lord to be stretched out to us. I trust you are feeling that need now as you read, and I am glad that you are feeling this need in your life. This will lead you to find your preservation in the Lord, who alone is able to keep us from falling and to glorify us with His Son.

# CHAPTER EIGHTEEN

# The Confirmed Christian

I want you to notice the security that Paul confidently expected for all the saints. He writes, "Who shalt also confirm you unto the end, that ye may be blameless in the day of our Lord Jesus Christ" (1 Cor.1:8). This is the kind of confirmation that is to be desired above all things. It presupposes that the saints have been made righteous, and it proposes to confirm them in righteousness to the end. It would be an awful thing to confirm someone in the ways of sin and error. Such a person could be a confirmed drunkard, confirmed liar, or confirmed thief. It would likewise be deplorable for a person to be confirmed in unbelief and ungodliness; but you, as a believer, have been confirmed in righteousness.

Divine confirmation can only be enjoyed by those to whom the grace of God has been manifested. It is the work of the Holy Spirit. He who gives faith will also strengthen and establish it. He who kindles love in us preserves it and increases its flame. What He helps us to understand at first, He causes us to know with greater clarity and certainty, as He continues to lead us, guide us, and instruct us. Holy acts are confirmed within us until they become regular habits, and holy feelings are confirmed until they become the abiding conditions of our lives.

Experience and practice confirm our beliefs and our resolutions. Our joys and our sorrows, as well as our successes and our failures, are sanctified in the same way that a tree is helped to root by the soft showers and the rough winds. The mind is instructed and its growing knowledge gathers reasons for persevering in goodness. The heart is comforted and in this way it is made to cling more closely to consoling truth. The grip grows tighter and the tread grows firmer, and the believer becomes more solid and steadfast.

This is not a merely natural growth, however, but it is as distinct a work of the Spirit as is conversion. The Lord will surely give it to those who are relying upon Him for eternal life. By His inward working in our lives He will deliver us from being as unstable as water and cause us to be rooted and grounded. This is part of the method by which He saves us; He builds us up into Christ Jesus and causes us to abide in Him.

Dear reader, you may daily look for this, and you will never be disappointed. The One in whom you have placed your trust will make you to become like a tree that is planted by the rivers of water—a fruitful tree with leaves that will not wither. (See Psa.1.)

### Confirmed unto the End

What a great strength it is to know that you are a confirmed Christian. Such a person is a comfort to the sorrowful and a help to the weak. Confirmed believers are true pillars in our Lord's house. They are not carried away by every wind of doctrine and they are not overthrown by sudden temptation. They are a great stay to others, and they act like anchors in times of trouble in the church. Dare to become like them. Don't fear, for the good Lord will work within you as He has worked in the lives of these stalwart believers. Though you are a babe in Christ now, one of these days you will become a leader in the church. Hope for this as a gift of God's grace, not as the wages of work or the product of your own energy or goodness.

The inspired apostle Paul speaks of those who are confirmed unto the end. He expected the grace of God to preserve them to the end of their lives, or until the return of the Lord Jesus. Indeed, he expected that the entire Church of Jesus Christ in every place and in every time would be kept to the end of the dispensation until the Lord Jesus, as the Bridegroom, would come to celebrate the wedding feast with His perfected Bride. All who are in Christ will be confirmed in Him until that illustrious day.

Jesus said, "Yet a little while, and the world seeth me no more; but ye see me: because I live, ye shall live also" (John 14:19). He also said, "My sheep hear my voice, and I know them, and they follow me: and I give unto them eternal life; and they shall never perish, neither shall any man pluck them out of my hand" (John 10:27-28).

He who has begun a good work in you will confirm it unto the day of Christ. (See Phil.1:6.) The work of grace in the soul is not a superficial sort of reformation. The life that is implanted within us as the new birth comes from a living and incorruptible seed that lives and abides forever. (See 1 Pet.1:23.)

The promises of God, which are made to all believers, are not transient promises; they will be fulfilled as the believer holds on to them until he or she enters into endless glory. We are kept by the power of God through faith unto salvation. This does not come about as the result of our own merit or strength, but it is a gift of undeserved favor and grace for those who believe. These are the ones who are preserved in Christ Jesus.

Jesus will not lose any sheep from His fold. No member of His body shall die. No gem of His treasure shall be missing in the day when He makes up His jewels. Dear reader, the salvation which is received by faith is not a thing that involves just months and years. It is eternal, and what is eternal can never come to an end!

### Blamelessness

Paul also declared that he expected the confirmed saints in Corinth to be "confirmed ... to the end *blameless*." This blamelessness is a precious part of our keeping. To be kept holy is better than to be merely kept safe. It is a dreadful thing when you see religious people blundering their way from one dishonor to another. Such people have simply not believed in the power of the Lord to make them blameless.

The lives of some professing Christians consist of a series of stumbles. They are never all the way down, yet they are seldom on their feet. This is not the way it should be, because a believer is invited to walk with God, and he or she can attain to steady perseverance in holiness through faith. This is what each of us should do.

The Lord is not only able to save us from hell, but He is also able to keep us from falling. We do not have to yield to temptation when it comes our way. The Bible says, "For sin shall not have dominion over you: for ye are not under the law, but under grace" (Rom.6:14). Always remember that the Lord is able to keep the feet of His saints, and He will do so if we will trust Him.

We do not need to defile our garments, for by His grace we can keep them unspotted from all worldly defilements. This is something we must do, because the Bible tells us that we shall not see the Lord without holiness.

The Apostle Paul prophesied that the Corinthian believers (and we, as well) would be preserved, "blameless in the day of our Lord Jesus Christ." The Revised Version of the Bible uses the word "unreproveable" instead of "blameless." A better rendering of this word might be "unimpeachable." God, grant that in that last great day we may stand free from all charges so that no one in the universe will be able to challenge our claim to be the redeemed of the Lord.

We do have sins and infirmities to mourn over, but these are not the kinds of faults that would put us outside of Christ. However, we must be clear of hypocrisy, deceit, hatred, and delight in sin, for these things would be fatal charges to us. Despite our failings, the Holy Spirit can work a spotless character within us before others. As He does so, we will be able to be like Daniel, who lived in such a way that he furnished no occasion for accusing tongues.

Multitudes of godly men and women have lived so transparently and consistently that none could accuse them or slander them. The Lord will be able to say of many believers, as He did of Job when Satan stood before Him, "Hast thou considered my servant Job, that there is none like him in the earth, a perfect and an upright man, one that feareth God, and escheweth evil?" (Job 1:8).

This is the triumph of the saints: to continue to follow the Lamb of God wherever He leads us and to maintain our integrity before the living God. May we never turn aside to crooked ways or give any cause for the adversary to accuse us. Of the true believer it has been written, "We know that whosoever is born of God sinneth not; but he that is begotten of God keepeth himself, and that wicked one toucheth him not" (1 John 5:18). May this verse describe each one of us.

Dear reader, even though you may just be beginning in the Christian life, the Lord can give you an irreproachable character. Even though you may have gone far into sin in your past life, the Lord can deliver you completely from the power of your former habits, and He can make you an example of virtue. He will not only make you moral, but He will make you abhor every false way and follow after all that is saintly. Don't doubt this, for He is able to accomplish these things in your life. The chief of sinners does not need find himself or herself behind the purest of the saints. Believe for this in your life, and according to your faith, it shall be done.

What wonderful joy there will be when we are found blameless on the Day of Judgment. A moving stanza from a great hymn helps us to see what that day will be like:

> Bold shall I stand in that great day,
> For who aught to my charge shall lay;
> While through Thy blood absolved I am,
> From sin's tremendous curse and shame?

What bliss it will be to enjoy such dauntless courage at the time when Heaven and Earth will flee away from the great Judge of all! This bliss shall be the experience of everyone who looks to the grace of God that is found in Christ Jesus. It shall be the experience of each one who wages continual war with all sin through the sacred might of the Lord.

# God Is Faithful

The hope that filled Paul's heart concerning the Corinthians provides full comfort to all who have fear of the future. Why did he believe that believers would be confirmed unto the end? Paul cites his reasons for this belief. He writes, "God is faithful, by whom ye were called unto the fellowship of his Son Jesus Christ our Lord" (1 Cor.1:9).

Notice that the apostle does not say, "*You* are faithful." This is for good reason, for the faithfulness of human beings is very unreliable and a mere vanity. Likewise, he does not say, "You have faithful ministers to lead and guide you; therefore, I trust that you will be safe." No, for if we were kept only by other people, we would not be well kept. Here's how the apostle puts it, "*God* is faithful." If we are to be found faithful, it is only because God is faithful.

The whole burden of our salvation rests upon the faithfulness of our covenant God. The whole matter of salvation is centered on the wonderful attribute of God's great faithfulness. As humans, we are as variable as the wind, frail as a spider's web, and weak as water. We can place no dependence upon our natural qualities or even our spiritual attainments. However, God remains faithful.

He is faithful in His love. He knows no variableness, neither shadow of turning. (See James 1:17.) He is faithful to His purpose; He never begins a work and leaves it undone. He is faithful in all His relationships; as a Father, He will never renounce His children. As a Friend, He will never deny His friends. As a Creator, He will never forsake the work of His hands. He is faithful to His promises, and He will never allow one of them to fail in a believer's life. He is faithful to His covenant, which He has made with us in Christ Jesus and has ratified with the blood of His sacrifice. He is faithful to His Son, and He will not allow His precious blood to have been spilled in vain. He is faithful to His people to whom He has promised eternal life and from whom He will never turn away.

The faithfulness of God is the foundation and cornerstone of our hope of final perseverance. The saints shall persevere in holiness, because God perseveres in grace. He perseveres in order to bless, and because this is true, believers persevere in being blessed. He continues to keep His people, and therefore they continue to keep His commandments. This is good solid ground upon which to rest, and it is delightfully consistent with the title of this book, *All of Grace*. It is God's free favor and infinite mercy which ring in the dawn of salvation, and the same sweet bells sound melodiously through the whole day of grace.

Therefore, I'm sure you are able to see that the only reasons for hoping that we shall be confirmed to the end and be found blameless at the last day are found in God, and in Him these reasons are exceedingly abundant.

These reasons are found in what God has done. He has gone so far in blessing us that it is not possible for Him to turn back. Paul reminds us that God has "... called [us] unto the fellowship of His Son Jesus Christ our Lord" (1 Cor.1:9). Has He called us? Then His call cannot be reversed, for "the gifts and calling of God are without repentance" (Rom.11:29). The Lord never turns away from the effectual call of His grace. The invariable rule of the divine procedure is revealed in this verse: "Moreover whom he did predestinate, them he also called: and whom he called, them he also justified: and whom he justified, them he also glorified" (Rom. 8:30).

There is a common call in which it was said that many are called, but few are chosen; but in this chapter we refer to another kind of call, a call which speaks of special love and necessitates the possession of that to which we are called. This calling is like the one that was given to Abraham and his seed, a calling that was irrevocable.

### Partnership with Jesus Christ

As we consider all that the Lord has done for us, we see strong reasons for our preservation and future glory, because He has called us into fellowship with His Son Jesus Christ. This means that we have a partnership with Jesus. Think on that for a moment—you are in partnership with Jesus Christ!

You have been called by divine grace and you have come into fellowship with the Lord Jesus Christ. Indeed, you have become a joint-owner with Him in all things! Henceforth, you are one with Him in the sight of the Most High! The Lord Jesus bore your sins in His own body on the tree, and He was made a curse for you. At the same time, He became your righteousness, so that you have been justified in and through Him.

You are Christ's and Christ is yours. As Adam stood for his descendants, Jesus stands for all who are in Him. As a husband and a wife are one, Jesus is one with all those who are united to Him by faith. This is a conjugal union that can never be broken. More than this, believers are members of the Body of Christ. As such, we are united to Him in a loving, living, and lasting union. God has called us into this union, fellowship, and partnership; and in so doing, He has given us the token and pledge that we shall be confirmed to the end.

If we were apart from Christ, we would be poor, perishable beings, and soon we would be taken away to destruction; but we are one with Jesus, so we have become partakers of His very nature, and we are endowed with His immortal life. (See 2 Pet.1:4.) Our destiny is linked with our Lord's destiny, and since we know that He will never perish, we know also that it is impossible for us to perish.

Think long and hard about your partnership with the Lord Jesus Christ, the Son of God. You have been called into this glorious partnership, and all your hope lies therein. You can never be poor while Jesus is rich, since you are a partner with Him, a member of the same firm, if you will. Want can never assail you, since you are a joint-proprietor with the One who is the Possessor of Heaven and earth. You can never fail, for though one of the partners in the firm is as poor as a church mouse and utterly bankrupt, the other Partner is inconceivably and inexhaustibly rich.

Through this amazing partnership you are lifted above the depression of the times in which you live, the changes that will come in the future, and the final shock when the end of all things takes place. The Lord has called you into fellowship with His Son Jesus Christ, and through that act and deed He has put you into a very safe place that is protected by an infallible Safeguard.

As a believer, you are one with Jesus. Therefore you are secure. You will be confirmed to the end until the day of His appearing. The Lord Jesus and the believing sinner are both in the same "boat." Unless Jesus sinks, the believer will never drown. Jesus has taken His redeemed into an abiding connection with himself. He is the Head of the corporation, and His name will never be dishonored, so we know we are secure from all failure.

With the utmost confidence, therefore, let us go forward into the unknown future linked eternally with Jesus. Let us lean on Him as our Beloved, and let us do so more and more. Our faithful God is an ever-flowing well of delight, and our fellowship with the Son of God is a full river of joy. Knowing these glorious things, we can never be discouraged. Instead, we shall cry with Paul: "For I am persuaded, that neither death, nor life, nor angels, nor principalities, nor powers, nor things present, nor things to come, nor height, nor depth, nor any other creature, shall be able to separate us from the love of God, which is in Christ Jesus our Lord" (Rom.8:38-39).

# CHAPTER TWENTY

# Concluding Thoughts

I trust you have followed me step by step through the pages and paragraphs of this book; but just reading a book has little value unless the truths on its pages are grasped, appropriated, and brought into the practical issues of life. If one went into a shop and saw a great deal of food, but did not eat it, he or she would remain hungry. Therefore, dear reader, I hope that you have devoured the truths of this book in an effort to satisfy your spiritual hunger and that you have actually laid hold on Jesus Christ.

I wrote this book in the hope of benefiting you and blessing you, and I have worked toward that end throughout. I am thinking of you as I write this concluding chapter. Indeed, I have stopped my writing temporarily in order to pray for you.

I have a firm conviction that you will receive a blessing from this book, so don't refuse what God has for you. Why should you refuse? God knows that I wrote every line in this book for your eternal good. In the Spirit, I now take you by the hand with a firm grasp. Do you feel the grip of my hand on yours?

There are tears in my eyes as I ask you these very important questions: Will you choose not to die? Will you think of your soul? Or will you perish through sheer carelessness?

Weigh these questions very carefully, for they speak of very solemn matters, as you know. Do not refuse Jesus, His love, His blood, and His salvation. Do not turn away from your Redeemer who died for you.

I believe that God has heard my prayers, and you, my reader, have been led to place your trust in the Lord Jesus and receive His salvation by grace. I also believe that He will keep you in the Christian life. Let Jesus be your all in all, and live and move in His free grace. There is no life that compares to the life that is lived in God's favor. To realize that everything good comes to you as a free gift from God will keep you from pride and from self-accusing despair. It will make your heart grow warm with grateful love and create a disposition within your soul that will be more acceptable to God than anything that could ever come from slavish fear.

Those who hope to be saved by trying to do their best know nothing of the glowing fervor and hallowed warmth that come from devout joy in God, which is the result of His great salvation that has been freely given to us according to His grace. The slavish spirit of "self-salvation" is no match for the joyous spirit of adoption that leads us to cry out to our true Father.

There is more real virtue in the least emotion of faith than can be found in any self-effort or religious ritual. Faith is spiritual, and God, who is a Spirit, delights in it for that reason. Years of saying prayers, going to church or chapel, and religious rites and ceremonies without the efficacious grace of God, could well be an abomination in the sight of God. A glance through the eye of true faith, however, is spiritual; and it is, therefore, very dear to your Father in Heaven.

Jesus said, "God is a Spirit: and they that worship him must worship him in spirit and in truth" (John 4:24). Look deep within. Who are you worshiping? Let God become the focal point of your worship and your spirit.

If you are saved, be on the watch for the souls of others. Your own heart cannot prosper unless it is filled with intense concern for others and a desire to bless them. The life of your soul is found in faith; its health lies in love. Do you desire to lead others to Jesus? If so, you are inspired by divine love. Let me take this opportunity to encourage you to get involved in the work of the Lord, which is the work of love. Begin at home. Visit your neighbors. Bring spiritual enlightenment to the village or city where you live. Scatter the Word of the Lord to all you come in contact with.

Reader, I want you to meet me in Heaven. Do not go down to hell! There is no coming back from that eternal abode of misery that is known as hell. Heaven's gate is open before you! Do not refuse God's pardon, which is provided by the full salvation that Jesus gives to all who trust in Him. Do not hesitate, and do not delay. It's time for action. Believe in Jesus now. Make your decision for Him full, immediate, and complete. Let it happen now.

Meet me in Heaven, for I look forward to meeting you there, and remember, it's *all of grace*.

# Glossary

**Atonement**: The word "atone" is derived from the phrase "at one." Consequently, it applies to someone who is in the state of being "at one with God." This describes a harmonious personal relationship with God that was made possible by Jesus' death on the cross. "To atone for" a wrong is to make restitution for it, and this is what Jesus did for us through His atoning death. The process of atonement is the process of reconciliation to the Father.

**Confession:**   Through confession one acknowledges his or her sin and helplessness. God promises, "If we confess our sins, he is faithful and just to forgive us our sins, and to cleanse us from all unrighteousness" (1 John 1:9).

**Contrition:**   Contrition is brokenness of heart. It stems from a root word that means "crushed." The Bible speaks of a broken heart (Ps.34:18), a broken spirit (Ps.51:17), and humility (Isa.57:15). All of these attributes are involved in true spiritual contrition.

**Grace:**   God's unmerited favor in our lives. It is something we can neither earn nor deserve; it a gift from God that He bestows on those He loves. Grace is at the heart of the gospel, because it stems from the Father's great love that was expressed through Jesus Christ. Paul writes, "For by grace are ye saved through faith; and that not of yourselves: it is the gift of God: not of works, lest any man should boast" (Eph.2:8-9).

**Iniquity:** Synonymous with sin, iniquity involves wickedness and evil. The Bible says, "For all have sinned, and come short of the glory of God" (Rom.3:23). Because this is true, Jesus took our iniquities upon himself when He died on the cross. He became the sacuÊfice for our sins.

**Justification:** This is one of our deepest needs, and it is a gift of God that was provided through the substitutionary death of Jesus Christ. One is justified through the repentance and faith that are provided through grace. It enables unrighteous people to become righteous in the sight of God. God views those who are justified as being "just as if" they had never sinned. Paul puts it this way, "For he hath made him to be sin for us, who knew no sin; that we might be made the righteousness of God in him" (2 Cor.5:21).

**Mercy:** This is one of God's central attributes, and it involves His love being actively expressed in the form of great help for His people. It is divine love being manifested through grace. Mercy always involves compassion and caring. It is the power of God at work in the world. The Bible says, "O give thanks unto the LORD; for he is good: for his mercy endureth for ever" (Ps.136:1).

**Propitiation:** Jesus Christ is the propitiation for our sins. (See 1 John 2:2.) This means that He died to cancel out the effects of our sins and our transgressions against God, and thereby He regained God's favor in our behalf. His death was the atoning sacrifice that enables us to have a personal relationship with our heavenly Father.

**Providence:** Divine providence is God's guidance and care in our lives. It is His power at work in our lives to help us and supply our needs. Paul writes, "But my God shall supply all your need according to his riches in glory by Christ Jesus" (Phil.4:19).

**Reconciliation:** This is a dominant theme of the Bible—the reconciliation of God to mankind, which brings us close to Him and enables us to have fellowship with Him. We were alienated from God by sin, but He has taken steps to overcome this alienation by sending His only begotten Son to die for us. The Bible says, "God was in Christ, reconciling the world unto himself, not imputing their trespasses unto them; and hath committed unto us the word of reconciliation" (2 Cor.5:20).

**Redemption:** To redeem something is to buy, get, or win it back. It also entails freeing someone from captivity. Unredeemed sinners are captives to sin and Satan, but Jesus is the Redeemer, who paid the penalty for our sin and made it possible for us to become members of the family of God. He reclaimed us for God. Paul writes, "For ye are bought with a price: therefore glorify God in your body, and in your spirit, which are God's" (1 Cor.6:20).

**Regeneration:** This is the new birth that comes to all who place their faith in Christ for salvation. They are born again, and this rebirth results in radical changes and transformations in their lives. The Bible says, "Therefore if any man be in Christ, he is a new creature: old things are passed away; behold, all things are become new" (2 Cor. 5:17). It is a total transformation.

**Remission:** Remission releases us from the guilt or penalty of sin. Our sins were remitted by Jesus' death on the cross. This means they were canceled out and eradicated. Jesus said, "For this is my blood of the new testament, which is shed for many for the remission of sins" (Matt. 26:28).

**Repentance:** Paul tells us that the goodness of God leads us to repentance. (See Rom. 2:4). Through His grace, God grants repentance to us. (See Acts 5:31). Repentance involves turning from sin and yielding one's life unreservedly to God.

**Revelation:** Spiritual revelation involves God revealing himself and His truths to receptive human beings. This revelation may come through the Bible, through the work of the Holy Spirit, through nature, and through experience. God takes the initiative in bringing revelation to us. Revelation results in greater spiritual understanding.

**Righteousness:** Righteousness involves a covenant relationship between God and His people. Those who accept Jesus Christ as their Savior and live for Him are righteous in the sight of God. Human beings have no righteousness of their own, but God "imputes righteousness" to us through faith. Paul writes, "Abraham believed God, and it was counted unto him for righteousness. Now to him that worketh is the reward not reckoned of grace, but of debt. But to him that worketh not, but believeth on him that justifieth the ungodly, his faith is counted for righteousness" (Rom.4:3-5). A righteous person acts in accord with divine commandments, and he or she is free from guilt or sin.

**Salvation:** When someone is saved, they are put into right relationship with God, and they have been delivered from the power and effects of sin. The Bible says, "For God so loved the world, that he gave his only begotten Son, that whosoever believeth in him should not perish, but have everlasting life. For God sent not his Son into the world to condemn the world; but that the world through him might be saved" (John 3:16-17).

**Sanctification:** Sanctification is a process through which we become more like God in His holiness, righteousness, and purity. It is conferred upon us by divine grace and it is perpetuated by divine grace as well.

*Study Guide*

This study guide will help you to understand Spurgeon's teachings about God's grace and to apply the teachings contained within this book to your own life. These questions may be used for group study, as well.

### Chapter One—A Personal Word to the Reader
1. What was Spurgeon's goal in writing this book?
2. In what way is this book like a fountain?
3. What is the role of grace in your life?
4. In order to hear the voice of the Lord, what must you avoid?

### Chapter Two—A Gift From God
1. What part does grace play in salvation?
2. What did Spurgeon say you would learn from this book?
3. The Lord has invited you to a personal conference with Him. What does He want to give to you?
4. How does faith come to our hearts?

### Chapter Three—God Justifies the Ungodly
1. What is the meaning of "justification"?
2. What enables us to be justified?
3. Why did Jesus Christ come into the world?

4. What is the "good news" that Spurgeon declares in this chapter?

5. Why must self-righteousness be avoided?

6. For what kinds of people are the great and effective remedies of grace and redemption designed?

7. Have you received God's forgiveness in your own life?

### Chapter Four—It Is God Who Justifies

1. Why do we need to be justified?

2. Who is the one Mediator between God and us?

3. What examples are there for you to follow in the Parable of the Prodigal Son?

4. What Bible verse did God speak to Spurgeon at a time in his life when he was burdened with guilt? How did this help him?

5. What did he learn from 2 Corinthians 4:21?

### Chapter Five—How Can a Just God Justify the Guilty?

1. What was Paul's answer to the title question of this chapter?

2. How can God be both just and the Justifier of the guilty?

3. What happened to the human race as a result of the Fall of Adam?

4. Why did Jesus have to suffer?

5. What does believing in Jesus entail?

### Chapter Six—Deliverance From Sinning

1. What is the key to becoming happy, restful, and spiritually healthy?

2. How can you rid yourself of sin?

3. What is the "double cure" to which Spurgeon refers?

4. What does God promise to you?

5. What should you do with the promises of God?

6. What is Spurgeon illustrating through the story of the cat and the sow?

7. What happens when you yield yourself to God's divine working?

## Chapter Seven—It Is by Grace Through Faith
1. What is the fountainhead of your salvation?
2. What is the channel of salvation?
3. In what way do you find new life?
4. Where is the source of all divine blessings found?

## Chapter Eight—What Is Faith?
1. What is faith?
2. What are the three elements of faith?
3. In what sense was Jesus made a curse for us?
4. What is the role of trust?

## Chapter Nine—Illustrations of Faith
1. Who enables you to see the truth?
2. From what does faith grow?
3. What is the root of obedience?
4. What does Spurgeon mean by "assured knowledge"?
5. What is God's compass for your life?

## Chapter Ten—Faith: the Channel of Salvation
1. What does faith do for us?
2. How does faith unite us to God?
3. What is the key to opening Heaven's gate?

## Chapter Eleven—I Can Do Nothing!
1. What has the Lord Jesus Christ become in your life?
2. What is the meaning of "repentance"?

3. What is both the object and cause of faith?

4. What does Romans 5:6 mean to you?

### Chapter Twelve—Ever-increasing Faith

1. What are some steps you should take to increase your faith?

2. How can the testimonies of other believers benefit you?

3. What is the role of God's authority in helping you to build your faith?

4. Have you yielded your life to the Lord?

### Chapter Thirteen—The Role of the Holy Spirit

1. In what ways does God work through providence?

2. What is the role of the Holy Spirit?

3. How does newness of life come to us?

### Chapter Fourteen—My Redeemer Lives!

1. Who is the hope of the guilty?

2. What does Jesus do for you?

3. In what sense is Jesus the "great Advocate"?

### Chapter Fifteen—Repentance and Forgiveness

1. What two elements join together in order to complete divine mercy in our lives?

2. What is the inseparable companion of faith?

3. What are the "two pillars" between which every person who comes to God must pass?

4. What two elements form the "warp and woof" of the fabric of real conversion?

### Chapter Sixteen—Repentance Is Possible, Available, and Acceptable

1. What makes repentance possible, available, and acceptable?
2. What happened after Jesus was exalted on High?
3. In what ways is Jesus at work in your life now?

### Chapter Seventeen—The Fear of Not Persevering to the End

1. How can we overcome the fear of not persevering to the end?
2. Who needs God's daily grace in their lives?
3. How can we overcome weariness?
4. How does Spurgeon describe "true religion"?

### Chapter Eighteen—The Confirmed Christian

1. Who is able to enjoy divine confirmation?
2. Into what is every believer confirmed?
3. What is the triumph of the saints?
4. What enables us to be kept blameless until the day of our Lord Jesus Christ?

### Chapter Nineteen—God Is Faithful

1. In what specific ways is God faithful to us?
2. What is the meaning of 2 Peter 1:4?
3. In what ways can you be lifted above the circumstances of the world?

### Chapter Twenty—Concluding Thoughts

1. How does one go about choosing not to die?
2. What do you think about your own soul?
3. Who are you worshiping?
4. Do you desire to lead others to Jesus?

# Index

## A

atonement 13, 33, 131
Atonement, the 28, 67, 99, 131

## B

Baptist Union xxvi, xxvii, xxviii
belief 47, 49
Bible 2, 8, 15, 19, 26, 36, 38, 47, 48, 50, 54, 57, 59, 65, 72,
     73, 79, 80, 118, 119, 131, 132, 133, 134, 135
Blood of Jesus 49, 54, 68, 81, 94, 96, 98
Bunyan, John 75

## C

Calvin xix, xxv, xxvi
Cambridge xii
Charles Spurgeon xiii, xix, xxix
Church of England ix, xi, xiii
Comforter 70
compassion 22, 43, 132
confession 65, 131
confidence 57, 58, 60, 75, 125

## D

devil 37, 72, 73, 76, 90
Down-Grade xxvi, xxvii, xxx

# Pure Gold Classics
## Timeless Truth in a Distinctive, Best-Selling Collection

An Expanding Collection of the Best-Loved Christian Classics of All Time.
## AVAILABLE AT FINE BOOKSTORES.
FOR MORE INFORMATION, VISIT WWW.BRIDGELOGOS.COM

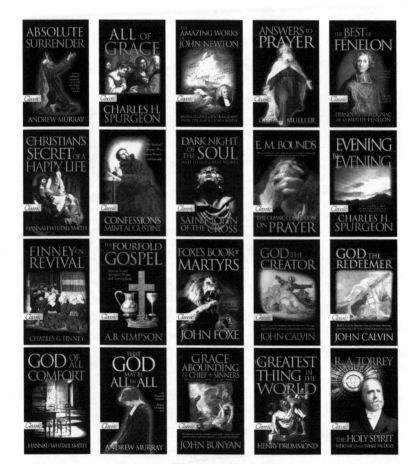

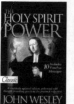
# THE HOLY SPIRIT POWER
Includes 10 Powerless Messages
**JOHN WESLEY**

# THE HOLY CATHOLIC CHURCH
**JOHN CALVIN**

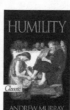
# HUMILITY
**ANDREW MURRAY**

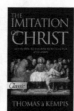
# THE IMITATION OF CHRIST
**THOMAS à KEMPIS**

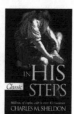
# IN HIS STEPS
**CHARLES M. SHELDON**

# INTERIOR CASTLE
**TERESA OF AVILA**

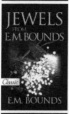
# JEWELS FROM E.M. BOUNDS
**E.M. BOUNDS**

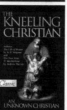
# THE KNEELING CHRISTIAN
**AN UNKNOWN CHRISTIAN**

# MADAME JEANNE GUYON

# MORNING BY MORNING
**CHARLES H. SPURGEON**

# OBTAINING THE GRACE OF CHRIST
**JOHN CALVIN**

# THE OVERCOMING LIFE
**D.L. MOODY**

# THE PILGRIM'S PROGRESS IN MODERN ENGLISH
**JOHN BUNYAN**

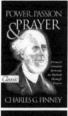
# POWER, PASSION & PRAYER
**CHARLES G. FINNEY**

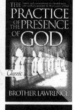
# THE PRACTICE OF THE PRESENCE OF GOD
**BROTHER LAWRENCE**

# SECRET POWER
**D.L. MOODY**

# A SERIOUS CALL TO A DEVOUT & HOLY LIFE
**WILLIAM LAW**

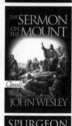
# THE SERMON ON THE MOUNT
**JOHN WESLEY**

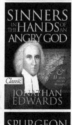
# SINNERS IN THE HANDS OF AN ANGRY GOD
**JONATHAN EDWARDS**

# THE SOVEREIGNTY OF GOD
**A.W. PINK**

# SPURGEON ON THE BLOOD OF CHRIST
**CHARLES H. SPURGEON**

# SPURGEON ON CHRIST
**CHARLES H. SPURGEON**

# SPURGEON ON GOD
**CHARLES H. SPURGEON**

# SPURGEON ON THE HOLY SPIRIT
**CHARLES H. SPURGEON**

# SPURGEON ON PRAYER
HOW TO CONVERSE WITH GOD
**CHARLES H. SPURGEON**

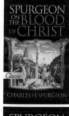
# SPURGEON ON THE PSALMS
BOOK ONE
Psalms 1 through Psalm 25
**CHARLES H. SPURGEON**

# SPURGEON ON THE PSALMS
BOOK TWO
Psalm 26 through Psalm 50
**CHARLES H. SPURGEON**

# SPURGEON ON THE PSALMS
BOOK THREE
Psalm 51 through Psalm 75
**CHARLES H. SPURGEON**

# TABLE TALK
**MARTIN LUTHER**

# TORREY ON PRAYER
THE POWER OF PRAYER & THE PRAYER OF POWER

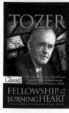
# TOZER
FELLOWSHIP OF THE BURNING HEART

# TOZER: MYSTERY OF THE HOLY SPIRIT
**A.W. TOZER**

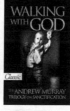
# WALKING WITH GOD
THE ANDREW MURRAY TRILOGY ON SANCTIFICATION

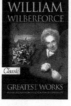
# WILLIAM WILBERFORCE
GREATEST WORKS

# WITH CHRIST IN THE SCHOOL OF PRAYER
**ANDREW MURRAY**